*Dedicated to the complete healing and restoration of those who*

*have been tragically wounded by friendly fire within the Church*

The Rock of Roseville
725 Vernon St., Roseville, CA
95678 U.S.A.
www.rockofroseville.com
www.rockspots.tv

Discovery Church
4402 S. Orange Ave
Orlando, FL 32806
www.discoverychurch.org

ISBN 10: 0-615-34568-9
ISBN 13: 978-0-615-34568-0

**FRANCIS ANFUSO** | **DAVID LOVELESS**

## ACKNOWLEDGMENT

Many marvelous representatives of Jesus have sacrificed and given of their time and talents to guide this book to completion.

First and foremost, our beautiful and godly wives were an invaluable help. Suzie aided Francis by brainstorming many aspects of this delicate topic, while Caron, a gifted author in her own right, assisted David in editing each of his chapters, helping David brainstorm chapter concepts and then exhaustively editing them. We would not be who we are today without decades of your wise counsel. You have our endless love and appreciation.

We are likewise indebted to our faithful assistants: Stephanie VanTassell and Robin Ragsdale. Each helped in numerous dimensions, which included: compiling the Church Wounds Survey and keeping us on schedule. The final editing of this book was in Stephanie's capable hands. She guided the project to its completion. There would be no book without Stephanie.

Additionally, two ladies were once again extremely helpful in the editing phase: Kathy Kunde, a dear friend for many years, and Betty Price, a gifted proof-reader and researcher. Many thanks!

The cover and graphics were completed by Hans Bennewitz, on time and with many an extra mile. I love working with you Hans. You're like a human sedative, always calming and reassuring.

Lastly, to the many hundreds of people who graciously filled out the online Church Wounds Survey. Thank you for opening your hearts to reveal the deep and painful hurts caused by others within the church. Our hope is that the value of your suffering will in some way impart life to others.

To each survey participant, we extend our prayers, love, and gratitude.

May the healing, Jesus accomplished, be imparted as you read this book.


Francis Anfuso and David Loveless

January 2010

# CONTENTS

Prologue—Francis Anfuso......................................................9

Prologue—David Loveless....................................................11

Introduction.....................................................................14

*Section One—The Wounded Church*

1    History of Church Wounds ............................................19

2    The Perfect Church ......................................................25

3    The Perfect Leader .......................................................33

*Section Two—Expectations*

4    Expectations ................................................................43

5    Misunderstandings.......................................................51

6    Offenses .....................................................................59

*Section Three—Hypocrisy*

7    Promises Unfulfilled.....................................................67

8    Hypocrisy ...................................................................75

9    Misrepresentation .......................................................83

10   Half-truths..................................................................91

*Section Four—Indiscretion*

11   Financial Impropriety.................................................101

12   Immorality.................................................................109

13   Inappropriate Behavior ..............................................117

14   Leader Insensitivities .................................................125

15   Believer Insensitivities ...............................................135

16   Misuse of Gifts of the Spirit (part A) ..........................141

     Misuse of Gifts of the Spirit (part B)...........................149

*Section Five—Controlling Spirit*

17    Pride ................................................................................155

18    Judgmentalism ................................................................163

19    Legalism ..........................................................................171

20    Possessiveness ................................................................179

21    Abuse of Authority .........................................................187

*Section Six—Elitism*

22    Self-centeredness ............................................................197

23    Favoritism .......................................................................203

24    Cliques ............................................................................211

25    Elitism .............................................................................217

*Section Seven—Church Politics*

26    Church Politics ...............................................................227

27    Doctrinal Divisions .........................................................235

28    Church Splits ..................................................................241

*Section Eight—Healing*

29    Fullness of Healing .........................................................251


Appendix .................................................................................257

Recommended Reading ...........................................................260

Recommended Viewing ...........................................................262

## PROLOGUE — FRANCIS ANFUSO

I have church wounds.

Some of my wounding came from growing up in a dead church. Watching a church service on TV that reminds me of my childhood, I have to turn it off before the remote becomes airborne.

My other church wounds are more pronounced and pervasive. They scarred me during two significant seasons since committing my life to Jesus in 1972.

The first season was as a young Christian. I was exposed to leadership insensitivities, hypocrisy, church politics, and abuse of authority. At one point, the pressure was so suffocating I nearly had a nervous breakdown. I would drive around town listening to worship music, just crying. Now, some 30 years later, God has significantly healed me from these events.

I traveled extensively throughout the body of Christ conducting seminars, conferences, and speaking in churches, when I accumulated my next volley of scarring. Though I had many wonderful times and met some incredibly godly and gracious people, by the time I finished my travels, I was significantly disheartened. The most grievous assault on my spirit came from witnessing firsthand the misrepresentation of Jesus and inappropriate behavior of Christian leaders. I never wanted to travel or minister in churches again unless I had complete confidence in the integrity of their leadership.

At times during my traveling ministry, I felt like I left in a get-away car, embarrassed that I supported a person or group that I could never, in good conscience, recommend. Often I would not return to those churches or ministries that were in some way misrepresenting God's Kingdom. Other times, I tried to bring balance to the errors I saw. Yet, I found it very hard to treat a spiritual infection or deception in a weekend, or even a week. There are always reasons for lack of health, whether natural or spiritual, and these are usually due to imbedded patterns that cause chronic sickness.

When I planted a church and began to pastor in 1997, I discovered my tendency to avoid other churches. I was elated that I didn't have to visit them anymore. This, of course, is not healthy. Over time I have seen the dysfunction of isolation. Therefore I am committed to being completely healed—no longer hiding.

My faith level has increased significantly over the last few years since I've been miraculously healed of a foundational dimension in my life—father wounds. I even wrote a book on the subject, *Father Wounds: Reclaiming Your Childhood.* After writing the book and preaching a series from its chapters, I found myself completely healed from a life-long heartache. My soul is now elated and so liberated I proudly display pictures of my father in my office.

But, such is not yet the case with church wounds.

I first heard about the "approach-avoidance" syndrome when I studied psychology in college. It went something like this: there are things that you need to do that you would rather not do because of the pain and inner battle they would produce. Candidly, this is how I feel about writing a book on the subject of church wounds. Part of me is as excited as I would be getting a root canal at the dentist. The other part of me knows that, although it's going to be painful, in the end I will be healed.

Francis Anfuso
The Rock of Roseville
Roseville, California
July 2009 (Written prior to the remaining *Church Wounds* chapters.)

## PROLOGUE — DAVID LOVELESS

The best times of my life have been in church. I found Jesus in a church and met my wife in one, too. At church I have shared fellowship so rich that even though it was two in the morning and our kids slept sprawled on the pews in pajamas, not one of us wanted to leave. I've felt moments when the glory of God hung so strong and pure on church leaders I ached to be just like them. A room full of bookshelves could not hold all the powerful, meaningful, beautiful experiences I've known in the Body of Christ. But there have been other times, dark times, when devastating events beat and robbed my trust blind, leaving me in a spiritual coma. The most shattering, gut-ripping blows have come at the hands of church people. Maybe yours have too.

I was 16 the night my view of the church was broadsided.

It was "prayer meeting" night, the time of the week in our church the truly committed were expected to attend. It started with a 'potluck' supper. No *Top Chef* here. Plates were piled with casseroles, coleslaw, and Kentucky Fried Chicken. Forever a famished, skinny kid, I loved it. This family-style feast was a valiant attempt to encourage the kind of kinship we read of in the second chapter of Acts. After dinner, kids retreated to classrooms while adults gathered in the sanctuary to sing songs and hear the third sermon of the week. In the few minutes actually devoted to prayer, we learned who was "shut in," whose aunt was in the hospital, and for a few brief moments, we signaled silently if we had a prayer so personal it could only be known as "unspoken."

But on the first Wednesday night of the month this all changed. Instead of preaching, the deacons called to order, complete with Sir Robert's Rules, an official church business meeting. A review of the monthly budget was the inspirational highlight. With the zeal of Sherlock Holmes, the entire adult population of committed believers would inspect every dime the pastor and staff spent the previous month. Anyone was free to inquire about a questionable or confusing expenditure. Whenever a member felt certain monies should not have been spent, which happened most months, the pastor and staff were called to give an account.

I was fascinated our church required a democratic vote to buy carpet for the nursery, decide if pencils where better than pens in the pews, or if there was need of a copier. Lengthy discussions launched into what kind of copier. Some asked, just for their information, how many copies per minute did the pastor and secretary actually need? Jesus didn't have a copier, and if *He* didn't have one, why did the pastor need one?

But this particular Wednesday night, the prayer/business meeting plunged deep south. Some were vexed that the pastor had authorized roof repairs. Shingles needed to be replaced. There were ongoing leaks. Our state had a rainy season longer than major league baseball's season. Since there was no one else to do it, the pastor found himself tending more to the buckets under leaks than to the needs of his flock.

I particularly remember one man's scolding face. In fact, I can perfectly remember his name, what he did for a living, and his role in the church. I can recall so many details you would think it was just last night instead of 39 years ago.

This man shot up, agitated, accusing the pastor of not doing his job—meaning bucket duty—and mishandling funds by authorizing the repair without a vote. His attack got personal and then cursing blasted from the man's mouth, like rapid machine gun fire aimed for the pastor, others shook their heads and agreed.

The look on my pastor's face is branded in my brain. It was like he had been shot. I'll also never forget it because my pastor was also my dad.

I bolted the building, livid and devastated. I ran all the way home. Nothing would persuade me to see those people again. I sobbed in my room, church-wrecked.

That night I decided church was not for me. Forget about church being a safe place to hear a dangerous message. Christians, I found out, were highly flammable, dangerous people. If this was a Christian life, count me out.

Now, nearly forty years later, guess where I am and what I do. I'm a pastor. Sometimes I still shake my head. My day job is pastoring Discovery Church in Orlando, Florida. I also pastor other pastors in places like California and Cape Town, South Africa. It's not only what I do, but what I love. I wouldn't trade anything for where I get to work and the people I'm called to serve. So what happened? How did I get from wounded church hater to zealous church champion?

From its launch, Christ knew His church would be far from perfect. He knew it would be populated with millions and millions of hyper-flawed humans like you and me. And He made numerous provisions for all her blunders, blemishes, and basket cases. Not only did He leave us promises and principles to meet the challenge of Christian community, He continues to supply personalized prescriptions for every kind of offense.

I know this is true. Since my first mortal wounding 39 years ago I've been hit countless times by spiritual shrapnel of every stripe and variety. But through it all, I've learned some practices that make all the difference. God has redeemed the pain. By tapping into His healing clinic, staffed by the power of the Holy Spirit who is on-call 24/7, I can actually love and lead the church that wounded my dad and me.

If you've been injured "in the name of Jesus," then join us on a journey of recovery. We not only want to identify with your church wounds, but show you how Christ has healed our own brokenness as well as countless others.


David Loveless
Discovery Church
Orlando, Florida
July 2009 (Written prior to the remaining *Church Wounds* chapters.)

## INTRODUCTION

Our long trek up, what we would consider, the Mt. Everest of church issues began with an online *Church Wounds Survey*. With well over 1,000 participants, our sampling was primarily drawn from the authors' two churches: The Rock of Roseville in Roseville, California and Discovery Church in Orlando, Florida.

Our results found that:

- 86% said they had church wounds.
- 70% said they have been significantly healed.
- 96% said they were willing to completely forgive anyone who hurt them in the past within the church.
- 63% said they had considered not going to church again because of their experience.

Additionally, 65 percent of those who took the survey believed church wounds to be prevalent or very prevalent among their friends and family. We are persuaded our findings are not an anomaly, but rather an accurate snapshot of a systemic dilemma ensnaring much of the Church in the Western world.

Frankly, because of scandalous exposures within both the Catholic and Protestant churches, church wounds are no longer a "dirty little secret" hidden in a closet. The visceral anger, once dormant, has now immerged with passion that has spread across the landscape.

## RULES OF ENGAGEMENT

As Jesus came to give us life, and that abundantly (John 10:10), our purpose in writing this book is to see God bring forth life from death. Therefore, here are seven *Rules of Engagement* that we committed to follow before one word was written.

1. We believe that much of the culture's hostility toward Christianity is caused by misrepresentations of the heart of God. (Matthew 18:7)

2. We understand that some wounds come from our own insecurities, and therefore make us more susceptible to certain wounding. (Jeremiah 17:9, Ephesians 4:32)

3. We sincerely respect each church leader's God-given spiritual anointing and authority, and have no desire to either make anyone look bad or demean offices within the Church. (1Chronicles 16:22, Romans 13:7)

4. We are persuaded that there is redemptive value in every wound or negative situation any of us will ever experience in life. What the enemy meant for evil God can redeem for the good. (Romans 8:28)

5. We realize that each of us could have fallen prey to many of the pitfalls we have experienced due to the mistakes and improprieties of others. (John 8:7)

6. We will never use the actual names of people, churches, or ministries. We do not want to embarrass anyone. (Proverbs 10:12, 1Peter 4:8)

7. Our purpose is not to pile on and play the "blame game." We earnestly desire every leader to be equipped to minister life to God's people and every wounded soul to be completely healed in order to move forward in their spiritual life. (Ephesians 4:11–17)

We have church wounds!

God will heal us!

Let's take the healing journey together.

# THE WOUNDED CHURCH

Section One

# HISTORY OF CHURCH WOUNDS

## CHAPTER ONE: *Francis Anfuso*

Jesus said, "But if anyone causes one of these little ones who trusts in Me to lose faith, it would be better for that person to be thrown into the sea with a large millstone tied around the neck." (Matthew 18:6)

Catastrophic abuses have been perpetrated in the name of Jesus Christ. Mention the Crusades, the Inquisition, and the Ku Klux Klan to any pastor and see him cringe. It seems trite to call these low points in church history. But whether done by genuine Christ-followers or not, they distorted truth and love. While these violations were eventually stopped by true Christians, the damage done in the name of Christ was far-reaching. Church wounds (more accurately, Church Crimes) have affected countries, races, families, and individuals.

Church wounds occur in two dimensions: *agendas* and *relationships* within the Church. First, we will briefly discuss *agendas*.

Much has been written about the abusive events that occurred in the name of the Judeo-Christian God. Still other atrocities were birthed in the fertile imagination of evil and attributed to Christians. Such fabrications are many and varied. Allegedly, Christians were in some way responsible for the Holocaust, the Jonestown mass suicide, the bombing of the Federal Building in Oklahoma City, and the Atlanta abortion clinic bombing. Asserting that followers of Jesus perpetrated any of these unthinkable acts is, in fact, an absurdity. Yet, proponents of this twisted reasoning claim Adolph Hitler, Jim Jones, Timothy McVeigh, and Eric Rudolph were all Christians.[1]

---

For a more detailed examination of these claims see the Appendix.

The actions of each of these self-deluded individuals prove that they had no relationship to the Christian faith whatsoever. True followers of Jesus will believe and do what He said, "Love your enemies! Do good to them! Then your reward from Heaven will be very great, and you will truly be acting as children of the Most High, for He is kind to the unthankful and to those who are wicked." (Luke 6:35) It is impossible to blatantly kill innocent people while claiming to be a follower of Jesus. Still, misrepresentations have caused rifts between people and the name of Jesus.

**DIRTY LAUNDRY**

While reconciliation must be made between the Church as a whole and entire generations who were wounded by the behavior of Christians, restoration must also take place within individuals.

The second dimension of church wounds, and the primary focus of this book, is *relational*. These are breaches in relationship, whether person-to-person or person-to-God, initiated by someone claiming to be a Christian. Some offenders seemed to have had a substantial relationship with Jesus, but have intentionally used or hurt people. However, the most common group of Christians who damaged others did so inadvertently.

They meant well, but messed up.

While professing to be followers of Jesus, they made errors in judgment, in word, or in deed, leaving a trail of pain that genuinely stumbled others.

Tragically, the pain did not stay in the pews. Research from the Barna Group, expounded on in the book *unChristian,* shows that young people, 16 to 29 years old who are presently outside of the church have lost much of their respect for the Christian faith. Two out of every five young outsiders (38 percent) claim to have a "bad impression of present-day Christianity." In addition, one-third of young outsiders said that Christianity represents a negative image with which they would not want to be associated.[2]

---

2    Kinnaman D, Lyons G. unChristian: What a New Generation Really Thinks about Christianity…
and Why It Matters. Grand Rapids, MI: Baker Publishing Group; 2007.

I don't know which surprised me more when reviewing the *Barna Survey*—learning that 87 percent of outsiders consider Christians judgmental or finding out 52 percent of churchgoers felt the same way. Our own *Church Wounds Survey* of over 1,000 people found that 42 percent of those surveyed were themselves hurt by the judgmentalism of other Christians.

Three out of every ten young outsiders said they have undergone negative experiences in churches and with Christians. Similarly, 85 percent of outsiders believe Christians are hypocritical, saying one thing and doing another, while 47 percent of those within the church felt the same way.[3]

Obviously, there is a problem. Perception has become, in some way, reality.

How many acute misrepresentations does it take to turn off a culture? It's been said, "no one cares how much we know, until they first know how much we care." Or, as the Bible so clearly articulates it, "While knowledge may make us feel important, it is love that really builds up the church." (1Corinthians 8:1b) It seems, in some cases, Christians resisting the entreating appeals of God's Spirit to love those around them have set this negative impression in motion.

Even though the scriptures teach and church history affirms, the true gospel of Jesus Christ is offensive to the natural mind (1Corinthians 2:14), people are not just offended by how we treat them. These are self-inflicted wounds, by Christians, on Christians.

Since it breaks God's heart, it should break ours.

As mentioned in the *Introduction*, our intention in writing this book is not to question the sincerity of followers of Jesus Christ, nor to undermine their gifts and callings, but rather to examine errors of judgment or conscious misdeeds. Though we genuinely seek understanding, healing, and restoration for all parties involved, we cannot sweep indiscretions under the rug. Nor can we wink at areas of church life and leadership that, frankly, grieve the heart of God and need to change.

---

3    Kinnaman D, Lyons G. unChristian: What a New Generation Really Thinks about Christianity… and Why It Matters. Grand Rapids, MI: Baker Publishing Group; 2007.

**FIRST WOUNDING**

With some imaginative license, we can trace the history of church wounds back to the Garden of Eden. The story line would go something like this:

A leader in spiritual authority (God) is accused by one of His leaders (the serpent) of not being fully forthright with members of His congregation (Adam and Eve). Though the accusation is false, it is believed and a church split ensues. To limit the spread of the rebellion, the senior pastor insists the two church members in question leave. His heart is broken. He has done nothing to overtly hurt them and everything possible to help them, yet they leave wounded and hurting. In time, the seed of deception within the expelled family spreads to their children: one son kills another (Cain kills Abel).

Though this particular scenario finds the members of the congregation at fault, as we have acknowledged, this is not always the case. Church leaders are often to blame.

Beyond the Christian Church, wounding takes place in all relationships, but some of those that are most hurtful occur within the faith-based community. Wounding within the Church is often more devastating for many reasons. Here are just a few.

DEEPER VULNERABILITY

Those who represent God are often given emotional access to the deepest part of a person's being: our spirit. When a breach or misrepresentation occurs at this level, people feel uncovered and unprotected. This type of wounding affects not just our perception of the individuals involved, but can skew our relationship with God Himself. We are His human representatives or, as the Bible says, "We are Christ's ambassadors, and God is using us to speak to you." (2Corinthians 5:20) Given such a serious responsibility, a breach can have lasting consequences.

## BROKEN TRUST

The deeper the relationship, the greater potential for hurt. All healthy relationships are in some way dependent upon trust. Broken trust, due to dishonesty or impropriety, assaults the very core of our being. When leaders and believers claim to represent a God of love, church wounds can often be most traumatic.

## EXPECTING PERFECTION

When promised a genuine representation of God's heart by a follower of Jesus, and significantly less is delivered, a person feels not just short-changed, but robbed. A violation has taken place. As one person in our *Church Wounds Survey* tragically lamented, "Every one of my family members is not attending church or does not have a relationship with God because of misrepresentations of God and the church." It breaks my heart to write it, but this was not a unique sentence; it was repeated over and over again by hundreds of respondents.

When Jesus said, in Matthew 18:6a (NASB), "whoever causes one of these little ones who believe in Me to *stumble*," the original language implies, "to put an impediment in the way, upon which another may trip and fall; to cause a person to begin to distrust and desert one whom he ought to trust and obey."

For such a brazen act of undermining someone else's faith, Jesus said, "it would be better for him to have a heavy millstone hung around his neck, and to be drowned in the depth of the sea." (Matthew 18:6b, NASB) Though I wish I could lessen the blow these words inflict upon the reader, I yield to the reality that Jesus doesn't need me to rationalize the intent of His words.

May God give us ears to hear the thoughts and intents of His heart.

Likewise, may we be willing to accept any responsibility that God's Spirit reveals to us as we read on.

We will certainly be glad we did.

# THE PERFECT CHURCH

## CHAPTER TWO: *Francis Anfuso*

"When that which is perfect has come, then that which is in part will be done away." (1Corinthians 13:10, NKJV)

"The only problem with finding the perfect church," someone once said, "is that our attending it would immediately ruin it."

Imperfection is a universal scourge—a birthmark unrestricted by age, nationality, economic status, or ethnicity. We all resist drowning in its incessant tug, but to no avail. Without God's intercession, we are incurable. But by His merciful kindness we can be redeemed.

My ability to process imperfection, in myself first and then in others, may very well determine my long-term spiritual health. Presenting myself as perfect has, ironically, caused those watching my life to lose respect for me. But admitting my mistakes and acknowledging when I have wounded others, confirms the obvious, but releases the empowering and healing grace of God.

I shudder when considering that everyone claiming to have a personal relationship with Jesus has made a blood-covenant to properly represent Him. The bar of authenticity is infinitely high. The Bible speaks of God in absolute terms, "He is the Rock; His work is perfect. Everything He does is just and fair. He is a faithful God who does no wrong; how just and upright He is!" (Deuteronomy 32:4) The essence of God is who we are called to be. Yet, living this highest of all callings often feels out of reach.

While "hostile outsiders" might have little compassion for Christians who fall short of this pristine picture of God, "healed insiders" tend to be more gracious. A willingness and capacity to forgive is perhaps the clearest indicator of a person's spiritual health. It accurately assesses his understanding of the depth of his own spiritual predicament, while releasing those equally impaired. Truly mature leaders recognize their weak points, and ask forgiveness when they fail.

Some *Church Wounds Survey* respondents provided great insight. One woman wrote, "I'm far from perfect, but I hide in Jesus when I'm feeling hurt from insensitivity." Another young lady added, "We are all flawed and imperfect. Hurt-filled people and a hurtful church is what sadly happens when you get a congregation of hurt people."

Nevertheless, the challenge of Jesus still remains, "But you are to be perfect, even as your Father in Heaven is perfect." (Matthew 5:48) In this case, the word perfect speaks of "reaching full maturity or completeness, lacking nothing related to our human integrity and virtue." God calls us out of the doldrums of imperfection into the balmy breeze of completeness. This can only be achieved by faithfully owning our shortcomings along the way. A *Church Wounds Survey* respondent clearly articulated this principle, "I have learned that in a healthy body of believers, not only do we all know we're not perfect, but we openly talk about our imperfections!"

I have often said, "I am a much better repenter than I am a Christian." This speaks to the reality that my only chance of walking in the Christ-likeness I long for is consistently admitting when I am not speaking or acting like Him. Though I have never lacked for opportunity, I have at times lacked the insight and courage to obediently walk the talk.

Irrespective of my poor responses to those around me, I am still responsible to clean up the hurts I have inflicted by my words and actions. Contrary to conventional wisdom, admitting my mistakes, even publicly, rarely causes people to think less of me. Though acknowledging I was an axe murderer would hardly clear the air, I have found that if my life is ever believed, or even believable, it is because people trust me—and this necessitates deep levels of forthrightness.

## THE ROAD TO PERFECTION

We each sense we will never be fully complete until we experience the pleasures of a great life. We have been created with an unquenchable longing for perfection. God alone can provide the love, joy, and peace we search for. Imperfect Earth pines for perfect Heaven.

This conviction did not begin with us. The quest for ideal life has been imprinted deep within our being because it is the heart of God. A perfect Creator designed a creation with the explicit purpose of becoming His flawless bride—an eternal partner, fashioned in His image and likeness.

In spite of all her many faults, God's plans for His Church remain exceedingly clear, "Christ loved the church and gave Himself for her to sanctify her by cleansing her with the washing of the water by the word, so that He may present the church to Himself as glorious—not having a stain or wrinkle, or any such blemish, but holy and blameless." (Ephesians 5:25b–27)

I can never embrace God's perfect plan for me until I know my own imperfection. The divine exchange takes place when I trade my foolishness for His faithfulness, my exaggerated sense of worth or worthlessness for the true value only God can give me. We are tempted to "proclaim our own goodness" (Proverbs 20:6) especially if attached to righteous appearances. Then, whether right or wrong, we come to believe that respect is due, as we in some way walk the higher ground. It is the right of passage for true Pharisees, but it is the beginning of the end for anyone genuinely desiring to know and live for Jesus.

Paul the Apostle articulated this most clearly when He wrote, "Your attitude should be the same that Christ Jesus had. Though He was God, He did not demand and cling to His rights as God. He made Himself nothing; He took the humble position of a slave and appeared in human form. And in human form He obediently humbled Himself even further by dying a criminal's death on a cross." (Philippians 2:5–8)

If the Son of God had to humble Himself daily, how much more do we? If Jesus intentionally lived in obscurity, choosing the lowest road, so must you and I. "You know how full of love and kindness our Lord Jesus Christ was. Though He was very rich, yet for your sakes He became poor, so that by His poverty He could make you rich." (2Corinthians 8:9)

**TRACKING THE PAIN**

Recently, a man I haven't seen in years wrote me a very broken and revealing email, dripping with church wounds. It began with, "I have only met two pastors in my life that would say 'I'm sorry'. One is dead, so you're it." Needless to say, being the surviving member of that tiny twosome added a greater sense of duty to my reply. I continue to offer comfort and counsel as he climbs out of a season of despair.

Some mature Christ-followers provided extraordinary insight in the *Church Wounds Survey*. They were able to see, in retrospect, the true value of their life experiences—even their most hurtful ones. One young lady wrote, "Growing up I realized that they [leaders] are human, and make mistakes. No one is perfect. Now, years later, I realize how God used that time [of being hurt in church] to allow my relationship with Him to grow—not to depend wholeheartedly on the faith of the people around me." Though this comment does not provide a license for any hurt inflicted, it clearly confirms that God redeems not only us, but also all that we have been through. The psalmist affirmed this principle, "The Lord will perfect that which concerns me." (Psalm 138:8, NKJV)

A young man's commentary in the *Church Wounds Survey* began sadly but ended on a profound note. "Every Christian I know has been hurt at least once by someone in the church. News flash—the only perfect One was nailed to the Cross!" The only opportunity to experience true forgiveness is to allow Christ's sacrifice on the Cross to become the permanent filter by which we process offenses.

Two mature women of God added their profound insights:

"Sadly, church wounds will always be among us because we are all sinful man. We all come in with expectations, thinking these people must float in the bathtub! Then reality hits and we are let down. It can be a small issue or a large one. But we as humans are not, and never will be, perfect. That is why we must always keep our eyes on Jesus as He will never fail us or forsake us."

"My relationship with God is not dependent on how I am treated by any church. I realize churches are made up of imperfect people, just like me. I am sure I have hurt people unknowingly through the years. I do think that some of the wounds I have received were unintentionally made by people who do not have a healthy view of God. I pray for those who have wounded others, that they will be touched by God and not continue relating in a way that brings about wounding."

## THE THEOLOGY OF ARROGANCE

The cockiness of man does not mirror the righteousness of God. In the past, I traveled within certain streams of churches that believed they had an "inside track" on truth. You'd get the impression that arrogance was a forgotten fruit of the Spirit. Whether this inappropriate attitude surfaced as the result of a professed "heightened revelation of scripture," or because of a supposed "extra-ordinary manifestation" of God's presence, it invariably led to an excess of hurts and wounds. If you didn't believe it, say it, or do it quite like someone else, you were seen as having missed the mark.

One of the more humorous demonstrations of this I'm-a-legend-in-my-own-mind outlook occurred when I was just beginning to travel and preach some thirty years ago. A pastor tried to persuade me that the Apostle Paul significantly lacked faith in certain areas of his teaching. Therefore, at long last, his group of churches was correcting Paul's error in judgment with their new doctrine. Yikes! Presuming your insight trumps the truth of God's Word is a scary thought.

We could derive false comfort from thinking we're superior to others. In the end, we will delude ourselves.

**HOW TO HEAL**

I remember when I was a hyper-energetic young boy; I was covered in the "trophies" of my rambunctious activity. I had a constant cycle of old and new cuts and bruises. Before the healing process was complete, I would often begin to pick at the wound. If my mother was in the room and caught me picking, she would say loudly in her thick New York accent, "Stop picking your scab! If you pick at it it's not going to heal as quickly, and it's going to leave a bigger scar!"

But like a typical independent-minded boy, I didn't listen. I simply saw scars as badges of honor from the battlefields of life. Consequently, now I have more pronounced scarring. Mom was right.

So too with church wounds! People pick at them their whole lives. Someone says or does something that stirs them up, and off they go—picking, spewing, and venting before God and man. Eventually they may heal, but with far more scars.

So, let this illustration become a filter as you read this book. The sooner you stop picking at your church wounds, the sooner you'll be healed.

Here are a few perspectives to remember as you read on:

- Everyone gets hurt relationally at some point in his or her life.
- As you look back into your past, realize that sometimes you were the recipient of pain, and sometimes you were the inflictor. Initially most people are more concerned about the pain they have received. As we allow God to heal us, our sadness for those we have hurt will appropriately increase.
- You need to decide how desperate you are to be healed. It will make all of the difference.
- God's perspective is the right perspective!
- You must resolve if you want to forever be a patient or, eventually, become a doctor.

We were created to be overcomers, capable of acknowledging each imperfection in our lives but forever vigilant to not allow any of them to conquer us. No loss is insurmountable. There are always opportunities for mid-course corrections.

Stay humble as you read, and healing will flow. As the psalmist contritely prayed, "The sacrifice You want is a broken spirit. A broken and repentant heart, O God, you will not despise." (Psalm 51:17)

Or as the Message paraphrase so eloquently states, "I learned God-worship when my pride was shattered. Heart-shattered lives ready for love don't for a moment escape God's notice." (Psalm 51:17, The Message)

Someone is watching as we read.

He promises to heal us as we respond well.

# THE
# PERFECT LEADER

CHAPTER THREE: *David Loveless*

Maybe you have read this email forward Want-Ad for the perfect minister:

*WANTED: The perfect minister who preaches exactly fifteen minutes. He condemns sins but never upsets anyone. He works from 8:00 AM until midnight and is also a janitor. He makes $50 a week, wears good clothes, buys good books, drives a good car, and gives about $50 weekly to the poor. He is 28 years old and has preached 30 years. He has a burning desire to work with teenagers and spends all of his time with senior citizens. The perfect minister smiles with a straight face because he has a sense of humor that keeps him seriously dedicated to his work. He makes 20 calls a day to congregation families, visits shut-ins and the hospitalized, and is always available in his office.*

*The perfect pastor is always in the next church over! If your current pastor does not measure up to him simply send this notice to six other churches that are tired of their pastor, too. Then bundle up your pastor and send him to the church at the top of the list. If everyone cooperates, in one week you will receive 1,643 new pastors.*

*One of them should be perfect.*

### VIEW FROM THE FAR SIDE

None of us really expect our pastors to be perfect. But we *do* prefer them as close to faultless as possible. Even though we know better, we are all guilty of hoisting certain men and women of God to lofty pedestals. This seems especially true if the primary view we have of the leader is from a distance.

As a college student, I greatly admired a pastor in our church. I'll call him Don. Don was passionate about Jesus and inviting people to know Him. I loved his strategic leadership style. He was fun to hang out with, an amazing athlete, and challenged me to go full out for the Lord. When the opportunity came to work with Don, I was all in! Then I encountered his weak side.

In meetings, Don could get easily irritated. Being a task-driven guy, he sometimes ran over people to get things done. If you messed up, he had an uncomfortable way of locking his eyes on your forehead.

When Don left to take a church in another city, was I a better leader having worked with him? You bet. But seeing him up close alerted me to the sometimes-ugly underbelly of leadership.

Leaders we watch from afar seem strikingly wise, the perfect picture of godly virtue and impeccable character, gifted as communicators, and winsome as gatherers. God calls these people to reach the world and encourage His Church. We read their books, hear their podcasts, watch their programs, and attend their conferences. But we don't know them personally. Many are sincerely dedicated Christ-followers. But if we really got the chance to be close to them, we might find, like Dorothy discovered in *The Wizard of Oz*, that the leaders behind the curtain are a little less great and powerful than we think they are. That pastor across town and the teacher on television have as many shortcomings as the leaders we know up close. The difference is in our distance.

As a young pastor, I looked for the best role models I could find. I saw Mike (not his real name) on Christian television, I sat in the front row at his conferences, and read all his books. Mike was the hottest thing in Church World and I wanted everything he had in Christ. Then, in a way only God could have arranged, I got to work closely with Mike. Whew wee! What a whirlwind. We ministered together in every setting imaginable, sometimes internationally. Those were heady days. But, in time, the curtain began unraveling. At first I laughed at his colorful lifestyle, excused his excesses and, often, abrasive personality. Eventually, accusations of financial and moral impropriety sobered my opinion and I resigned from Mike's team. From working closely with Mike, I discovered not only was he the amazing man of God I believed, he had a certified sin-torched heart like mine and was not the fourth person of the Trinity after all.

## LONGING FOR LEADERS

Throughout Scripture, people looked for the perfect leader. The Israelites begged God to give them a king. Because other nations had kings they believed they were missing out. A great ruler would fix everything. We know how that turned out.

And when John the Baptist showed up, his followers questioned if he was the savior they were seeking:

> *Now this was John's testimony when the Jews of Jerusalem sent priests and Levites to ask him who he was. He did not fail to confess, but confessed freely, "I am not the Christ." They asked him, "Then who are you? Are you Elijah?" He said, "I am not." "Are you the Prophet?" He answered, "No." Finally they said, "Who are you? Give us an answer to take back to those who sent us. What do you say about yourself?" John replied in the words of Isaiah the prophet, "I am the voice of one calling in the desert, 'Make straight the way for the Lord.' I baptize with water," John replied, "but among you stands one you do not know. He is the one who comes after me, the thongs of whose sandals I am not worthy to untie." (John 1:19–30, 35, NIV)*

## SAVIORS OR SERVANTS?

All of us at some point want a leader to act like a savior. Some leaders think they can. We see this every day in sports, politics, relationships, with parents and even churches. I admit as a husband, father and leader there were many times I have donned the silk cape of a situational savior.

This was painfully revealed to me on a red-eye flight home from Dallas with my adult son, Josh. I had seen a video he used for a teaching moment where he alluded to his childhood. He said there were certain things he had been taught and experienced that greatly confused his view of God and the Church. At the time I thought he was stretching things to make a point. But just in case, at 30,000 feet, I decided to ask him about it.

Bad idea.

For the next hour Josh was brutally honest about theological decisions I had made as "Pastor Dad" that brought about deep confusion and years of questioning. I sat stupefied. How had I not known this? How could I have hurt my son in this way?

It was a cleansing talk for Josh and a punch to the gut for me. With tears I asked his forgiveness and he was good enough to forgive me. As we prepared to land I turned my face to the window and sobbed. I had wounded my own son in the area I had passionately worked his entire life to model well for him.

Leaving the plane, still shaken, I hugged Josh repeating again how sorry I was I had done such a terrible job. Then he said, "Dad, would you just get over it! I happen to believe I have one of the best dads on the planet and was led by one of the finest leaders I know. It's just that you made some mistakes and you can't handle that. You've always wanted to be perfect and you aren't. Just accept it—you're imperfect!"

My son spoke truth. And this profound yet simple truth would set me free.

## LEADERS WITH A LIMP

Most Christian leaders I know privately grieve when they see they have missed the mark. Believe me, they are painfully aware of their weaknesses. Whether it is relational, vocational, or character weakness, they carry it with them every day. And if a spouse or a church member doesn't remind them of it, be sure the enemy will find a way to keep it ever before them.

That's how I was feeling in 1995 during a difficult ministry season. Here's what I wrote in my journal:

*"Yesterday, I went to see Jean, my head-checker, for the second time. I am messed up. I have always felt like I am responsible for the care and accomplishment of others. Where did the illusion that I can be responsible for everything and everyone come from? My burnout comes from living this illusion. I must come to reality: I am not the answer. I am not Superman. And I thought I could be. What I need to do is to show up in the relationships and responsibilities of my life and just be me—perhaps*

*for the first time. I can't make that much of a difference. Neither can anyone one else. How freeing it is to just show up! Only God can make a huge difference and create increase in people's lives. I can't change all the issues with people I live with and work with. I just do my part but the actual change is between them and God. Otherwise, I end up exhausted and resentful. I was programmed to take responsibility for things that weren't mine. My role should have been helping people take care of themselves instead of relying on me to be the answer."*

One of the most difficult times of my ministry was when I had disappointed a lot of people with decisions I made for the church. Conversations got heated and many, including staff, left our church. For months God humbled and disciplined me in areas of my heart that needed an overhaul. I had been called to help heal the hurting, but God had me on the spiritual operating table. When I finally got off, I was freshly aware of a new role—that of a wounded healer.

Abraham was a great leader but he said and did things that embarrass me to no end. Moses was a great leader but he said and did things that embarrass me too. David was a great leader; Peter was a great leader…same story.

The Lord gave grace to these failed, ancient leaders He still so powerfully used. I wonder—can we also extend grace to the good men and women who have sincere hearts and holy intentions but lead us with limps today?

## WHY DO WE NEED SPIRITUAL LEADERS?

God clearly assigns spiritual leaders to cast spiritual vision. They keep our eyes on the prize, encourage, teach, counsel, and model Christ-like lives, though they are flawed examples (or "samples") of godly living. Any leader we submit to should be visibly, humbly seeking to reflect the abundant life of Christ. Not its totality, but its essence.

Don't pastors' limitations negate their teaching, their mission, and their example? No. God allows the flaws to surface, like Paul's thorns in the flesh, as obvious reminders to them and to us they are ever-dependent on Him.

### WHAT DOES PROPER REGARD FOR SPIRITUAL LEADERS LOOK LIKE?

As Christians, we often either revere our pastors too much or respect them too little. Scripture is clear: ultimate reverence is reserved only for the Lord. But it also teaches that those called by God to labor among us in the church are worthy of "double honor."

> *The elders who direct the affairs of the church well are worthy of double honor, especially those whose work is preaching and teaching. (1 Timothy 5:17, NIV)*

In Hebrews 13:1 we are encouraged to, "Remember your leaders, who spoke the word of God to you. Consider the outcome of their way of life and imitate their faith." The key phrase is, *consider the outcome of their way of life.* Jesus said we would know people by the fruit of their lives. Observe a leader's character and eagerness to lead a Christ-centered life. If they humbly exhibit fruitful, faithful public and private lives, we are exhorted to submit to their leadership. "Obey your leaders and submit to their authority. They keep watch over you as men who must give an account. Obey them so that their work will be a joy, not a burden, for that would be of no advantage to you." (Hebrews 13:17, NIV)

### WHAT SHOULD I DO IF A LEADER HAS WRONGED ME?

Few situations are more devastating, disillusioning, and faith-robbing than having our trust broken by a spiritual leader. No true leader in Christ's Body wants to be responsible for breaking someone's trust. Depending on the offense, we can feel intimidated, ashamed, or angry. Jesus warns spiritual leaders of the consequences they face for the misuse of the sacred charge given them by God and that God will surely judge any unrepentant leader.

But in Matthew 18, He also outlines his path for reconciliation with everyone, including fallen spiritual leaders. With a humble, prayerful heart, follow each of those steps, then consider the approach one woman in our *Church Wounds Survey* practices:

*"Where trust has been broken, I am quick to forgive and restore the relationship but know that rebuilding trust is earned over time. I have adopted an expression from John Townsend in his book Loving People, 'Forgiveness is about the past, restoration about the present, and trust is about the future.'"*

If trust continues to be broken with a leader, ask God to direct you to one more trustworthy. However, if you have several trust fractures with multiple leaders you may have issues with authority. If you sense this is true, let a wise, godly friend or Christian counselor help you work through this.

But if you have experienced serious emotional or physical abuse from a pastor or church leader do not dismiss your pain. Please know your Heavenly Father grieves this debilitating church wound. Seek safe emotional healing with a trained Christian therapist, preferably one who has experience processing this heart-breaking but utterly healable kind of injury, as soon as possible.[4]

One man in his thirties who took our survey had this encouragement to offer: "Everyone is under construction no matter who they are, where they come from, or what level of authority they may have over you. Pick your leaders carefully. Stay humble. Don't follow leaders who have no earthly accountability, who never include themselves in calls to repentance."

I got healed of my church wound when I let leaders be fully human. I accepted the fact, as disappointing as it was at times, that these leaders were really more like me than I first thought; all leaders are capable of sin. And yet their fallibility did not negate the gifts God had given them to use for His glory, nor did it erase many of the massive contributions they could make to my spiritual life.

Let's not shoot our messengers. Instead, let us commit to bless them and pray for them to be victorious in every area of their lives.

---

4    For help in finding a local Christian counselor, please contact the American Association of Christian Counselors at 800.526.8673 or visit their website at www.aacc.net.

# EXPECTATIONS

*Section Two*

# EXPECTATIONS

## CHAPTER FOUR: *David Loveless*

Several years ago, a woman sat in my office angry and upset. She was leaving our church. She was not leaving over a fight with her spouse, friend, or small group leader. The woman was torched with me.

I had known her for a long time. I presided over her wedding. Later I helped her and her husband through challenging marital issues. They seemed significantly helped and nurtured in our church. I loved them, was always happy to see them, and often told them how proud I was of their spiritual and relational growth.

So what had gone wrong?

I was a no show at a critical time in her life.

The woman's mother had suddenly died. From our experiences together, she and her husband felt close to me but I was unable to be there for them. Instead I asked one of our most thoughtful, experienced pastors to walk with them in their grief and help with the funeral. But the woman could not forgive my lack of care.

I told her how sorry I was for her loss and how I wished I could have been there or had at least called. We were in one of the fastest growth seasons of our church's history. It had become increasingly impossible to personally attend our members as I once could. I was simply unable to meet everyone's needs. She left our church, her view of me in shreds.

Unlike any other entity in history, the Church is a greenhouse for every variety of expectation. Why? Because the Church is founded on the Bible which contains more than 7,000 promises! The Church teaches those scriptures and seeks to exemplify them. However, only one Person made those promises to us and only that Person has the ability to deliver 100% of the time.

## GREAT EXPECTATIONS

Some common expectations of church go like this:

- We expect to get spiritually fed and relationally connected.

- We anticipate that small group leaders, children's volunteers, worship and student pastors will serve us faithfully.

- We assume someone will visit us in the hospital and that someone will be very high on our church's spiritual food chain.

- We hope our leaders will preach like Paul, write like Luke, lead like Joshua, envision like Nehemiah, and listen like Mary. They don't have to be as sinless as Jesus, but come pretty close.

- We expect people who go to church to act like they go to church. If a person carries a Bible, shouldn't they live like they know what it says?

- We presume that if we have faithfully served our church for at least six months, we deserve special treatment before the folks who just showed last week.

Expectations are born when we believe people will do what we think they should or what we perceive they promised. And sometimes we feel worthy of attention, favor, or special treatment.

Jesus spoke of our tendency toward this:

*When He noticed how the guests picked the places of honor at the table, He told them this parable: When someone invites you to a wedding feast, do not take the place of honor, for a person more distinguished than you may have been invited. If so, the host who invited both of you will come and say to you, 'Give this man your seat.' Then, humiliated, you will have to take the least important place. But when you are invited, take the lowest place, so that when your host comes, he will say to you, 'Friend, move up to a better place.' Then you will be honored in the presence of all your fellow guests. For everyone who exalts himself will be humbled, and he who humbles himself will be exalted. (Luke 14:7–11)*

## WHAT IS GOING ON?

In churches several dynamics converge. You have leaders who genuinely want to help people. Their desire is born of spiritual gifts, passions, the unction of the Holy Spirit, and seeing needs in others. They want to shepherd. They want to serve. They truly care. Sometimes leaders make promises. They try to describe what they believe they can do for people and do their best to follow through.

You also have people who demonstrate spiritual progress. They share testimonies of God's work in their lives saying things like, "I've won a decisive victory." "God healed my anger." "I'm a new person now." What they mean is that they have won *a* battle, in a series of many to come. Those listening expect these "victory" folks to cease struggling in the areas they have conquered.

Then there is the perception of the whole Church, the big "C" Church, before the world. Most on the outside, and many on the inside, believe that people who go to church are more holy. By participating in various services, groups and ministries, churchgoers are somehow more righteous and fully surrendered to God. Yet we know, *from our own experience*, church attendance is just a step in the long journey of surrender and obedience to the ways of Jesus.

These volatile dynamics can cause serious wounding. One woman from our survey shared this: "During my divorce I sought help from a church and was put on a waiting list. I would get a call saying, 'We will pray for you.' Sometimes people need more."

Another woman in her twenties said, "I had a mental health problem and a spiritual problem that I took to my minister. Instead of counseling me personally, she referred me to a counselor outside our church. She knew I was unemployed and could not afford these services. It bothered me that she just brushed me off."

"The entire pastoral team knew we'd lost a baby and a cherished pet," a forty-something woman said. "We never received an email, phone call, or anything. During our ten years at that church they always stressed the need to be there for one another. Yeah right."

### DID HE SAY *SINNERS* IN THE CHURCH?

*While Jesus was having dinner at Matthew's house, many tax collectors and "sinners" came and ate with Him and His disciples. When the Pharisees saw this, they asked His disciples, "Why does your teacher eat with tax collectors and 'sinners?'" On hearing this, Jesus said, "It is not the healthy who need a doctor, but the sick. But go and learn what this means: 'I desire mercy, not sacrifice.' For I have not come to call the righteous, but sinners." (Matthew 9:10–13, NIV)*

Jesus affirmed there would be sinners in His Church. Even He did not live up to everyone's expectations of righteousness! Many followers expected Jesus to act one way but He acted just the opposite. They had wrong expectations of Him, both as leader and Savior. There was a disconnect between what they wanted Jesus to do and His assignment from His Father. For many, Jesus was a huge disappointment.

In Matthew 20:1–16, He taught about how different the Kingdom of God operates.

*For the kingdom of heaven is like a landowner who went out early in the morning to hire men to work in his vineyard. He agreed to pay them a denarius for the day and sent them into his vineyard...He went out again about the sixth hour and the ninth hour and did the same thing. About the eleventh hour he went out and found still others standing around. He asked them, "Why have you been standing here all day long doing nothing?" "Because no one has hired us," they answered. He said to them, "You also go and work in my vineyard." When evening came, the owner of the vineyard said to his foreman, "Call the workers and pay them their wages, beginning with the last ones hired and going on to the first." The workers who were hired about the eleventh hour came and each received a denarius. So when those came who were hired first, they expected to receive more. But each one of them also received a denarius. When they received it, they began to grumble against the landowner... But he answered one of them, "Friend, I am not being unfair to you. Didn't you agree to work for a denarius? Don't I have the right to do what I want with my own money? Or are you envious because I am generous?" So the last will be first, and the first will be last.*

Part of the failure of unmet expectations comes from living in a two-world system. We cannot function well in God's Kingdom while clinging to worldly assumptions.

The Church, the only earthly representation of Jesus, has let a lot of people down. Because of this, some have questioned their faith or lost interest in pursuing a godly life. Sometimes a believer or fellowship's behavior has been so unbecoming, I want to revoke their "Christian card."

Still, we must choose to not be offended.

## ADJUST YOUR 'EXPECTOR'

One of my favorite scenes from the classic baseball movie *Field of Dreams* is when a struggling young farmer plays an illusionary game of catch with his deceased father on the baseball field he built in his cornfield. At one point the father looks around the field and asks, "Is this heaven?" His son smiles and answers, "No, Dad. This is Iowa."

We all need daily reminders that where we live, work, and worship is only "Iowa." Though, at times, it can feel like heaven, we will always land south of paradise. I'm learning to adjust what I expect from people. Even though I'm a positive person with a sizable gift of faith, disappointment in others is part of my human condition. I also know I have failed, will fail, and *am* failing people myself. But when this happens, I seek to acknowledge before God that I am, like all of us, flawed. We are fallen humans doing our best to copy the life of Christ.

We can expect that, in most cases, people try hard and mean well. There will always be a gap between what we might need from others and what they are capable of delivering. The good news is that if we let Him, we *can expect* the Perfect One, Jesus, to cover the lack in every relationship.

A scripture I find comfort in is this: "Find rest, O my soul, in GOD ALONE; my hope comes from Him. HE ALONE is my rock and my salvation; He is my fortress, I will not be shaken." (Psalm 62:5–6, NIV; emphasis mine)

Make allowance for human limitations. Expect that some will not always:

- Remember your name or the last conversation you had together.
- Be able (for good and selfish reasons) to attend the party you are hosting.
- Include you on their "Friends List" though you have mutual friends and frequent the same social network.

It is reasonable to expect church leaders to:

- Do their best to love God and care about people.
- Develop their gifts and leverage them for the greatest service.
- Respond in some form, within a specified time, to communication.
- Be available for a brief meeting in a church lobby or other public setting when a free moment arises.
- Lead with integrity and ask for forgiveness.
- Be removed from their position (but not the church) if they repeatedly violate moral and spiritual standards of scripture and refuse correction.
- Be accountable to overseers for their life and ministry.

Expect no one but the Lord Jesus to be there for you all the time.

## RELEASING THOSE WHO LET US DOWN

Even when we try not to get offended, we still do. In some situations it can feel like we've been hurled off a cliff without a parachute. I've lost count of the times I've felt let down by others. If I allow, I can quickly revisit the hurt, the betrayal, and the huge discouragements I have experienced.

On the flip side, I have also seen much healing.

Recently, a person approached me in the lobby of our church and said, "Pastor David, do you see that man over there? He used to be my pastor in another church. He and the leaders wounded a lot of people by mishandling a conflict. Now, he is coming to this church and seems like a new person. I am coming to this church and being healed as well. Isn't God good?"

With God all things are possible.

"Forgive us our debts as we forgive those who are in debt to us," is as relevant and needed in our churches today as it was when Jesus first uttered the words.

Sometimes I am able to forgive quickly and mean it. In those times I am able to get alone and invite the Holy Spirit to give me grace only He can provide. This unlocks those who have hurt me from an emotional prison. The longer I withhold forgiveness, the more power the situation has to continue to hurt me. The sooner I release the "prisoner" from captivity—that place I keep punishing and telling him off in my mind—the quicker I can be free of the pain myself.

But there are times we need a trusted friend, counselor, or small group to pray over and minister to us so we can find strength to let our disappointment go. It's okay to need prayer. I have asked for prayer many times. Never let fear or pride keep you in bondage. The power of Jesus meeting two or more in this way is electric.

Has someone in the Body of Christ wounded you? Do you still carry bitterness or resentment for unmet expectations? What do you need to do to release them?

Recently, I saw the woman who came to see me that day in my office. She and her husband sat beaming as I taught a message at our church. They returned to our church some time ago and we joyfully reconciled. God has done great healing in them and I believe our experience has made me a better leader. It took each of us drawing on grace for a better day to see this happen.

# MISUNDERSTANDINGS

## CHAPTER FIVE: *Francis Anfuso*

*"A mistake is to commit a misunderstanding."* —Bob Dylan

Ellison was stabbed numerous times during an Election Day brawl. It was reported to be the result of a long-standing feud that started over a hog. We're not talking about a motorcycle here, but an actual animal: a pig. The decision as to who owned the hog was left to a preacher, who also served as a local magistrate, and just happened to be a cousin of one of the plaintiffs. The verdict far from settled the issue, leaving hard feelings on both sides.

Years went by. Other incidents fanned the flames of mutual animosity.

On the Election Day that Ellison was assaulted, one of his attackers named Tolbert approached him saying repeatedly, "I'm hell on earth!" Ellison cursed at Tolbert, who then pulled out a knife and began to slash Ellison. Tolbert's two brothers soon joined in.

The three brothers were arrested and charged with attempted murder. When he heard of the incident, the leader of Ellison's clan proposed leaving their punishment up to the authorities. But many family members wanted to enact the Old Testament admonition, "an eye for an eye." (Exodus 21:23–24)

Twenty or more of Ellison's relatives stalked the three criminals determined that if Ellison died, they would execute judgment. The next day when he finally succumbed to his injuries, the three were ambushed and brutally put to death, each shot numerous times.

Hard feelings and multiple murders continued for a dozen or more years. Such were the sordid beginnings of what has been called the greatest feud in American history: the infamous 1880s vendetta between the Hatfields and the McCoys.

Most misunderstandings do not end with bloodshed. However, left unchecked, misunderstandings can maim and even kill our most cherished relationships.

## TONGUE LASHINGS

A pastor makes a flippant comment from the pulpit. Someone in the congregation takes it to heart, is offended, and leaves the church.

A church leader, during a conversation, makes a judgmental statement. It hurts and disheartens the one they are talking with. Trust is broken.

An insensitive, critical email is sent. The consequence of the wording is not considered. The recipient is hurt and loses respect for the sender.

Unintentional wounds can injure just as much as premeditated ones.

I would define effective communication as "saying what can be clearly understood." We may have gotten it off our chest, but if its intended meaning failed to bring understanding, we have not communicated.

Our desire for healing can be no greater than our commitment to understand.

If we are prone to distrust, then misunderstandings will be more commonplace. I have seen identical situations produce opposite responses. One person overlooks flippant words while another allows careless comments to cause a breach and offense. It is not uncommon that even years later, the wounded party can rehearse the event and relive the pain it produced.

Expressions like, "he's a bull in a china shop," "when you're around her you feel like you have to walk on eggshells," or even "his foot's usually in his mouth," are familiar to all of us because misunderstandings are so common.

We have each experienced the consequence of indiscretion.

Discretion has been defined as, "the ability to avoid words, actions, and attitudes which could result in undesirable consequences."[5] A lack of discretion can kill a relationship.

A Korean proverb states, "Below the tongue, there is an ax hidden." Or, as The Message Bible says, "Words kill, words give life; they're either poison or fruit—you choose." (Proverbs 18:21)

The Bible affirms, "Those who control their tongue will have a long life; a quick retort can ruin everything," (Proverbs 13:13) and, "no one can tame the tongue. It is an uncontrollable evil, full of deadly poison." (James 3:8)

## THOUGHTLESS PROPOSAL

All communication is not created equal. When I proposed to my wife, Suzie, I set up an appointment to meet with her. While attempting to express my deep love and admiration, I inadvertently blurted, "Out of all the livestock, you're the fairest of them all."

Am I kidding?

I wish I was!

Thirty-four years later it's still embarrassing to think about.

Thank God the intent of my affection for her overshadowed this absolutely unromantic statement. But trust me, no amount of time has made it flow better. Though funny now, in retrospect it was not what I wanted to say and could easily have been offensive. I'm sure my daughters will share this stunning faux pas with their own children and grandchildren for generations to come.

Someone once said, "The world only goes round by misunderstanding."[6] Though this expression is obviously a cynical view of life, it demonstrates how prevalent and potent misunderstandings are.

---

5    Gothard, B. Institute in Basic Life Principles. Character Qualities.
     Available at http://billgothard.com/bill/teaching/characterqualities. Last accessed January 3, 2010.

6    Charles Pierre Baudelaire (1821–1867) was an influential nineteenth century French poet,
     critic, and acclaimed translator.

A twenty-something *Church Wounds Survey* participant from England had a particularly hurtful encounter at her church. She wrote, "I was perceived to be in the wrong, and no-one bothered to find out whether it was a right perception. Insensitive to my needs and emotions—I was treated as an employee and not as a member of the congregation. Wrong judgments were made about my character, but no one asked me any questions about it—they spoke it as truth."

Though forgiveness and healing came later, this "close encounter of the insensitive kind" could have taken her out…forever.

A mature Christian woman commented in our survey, "People are fallible. They have wounds and misunderstandings." Though she believed she was completely healed of her church wounds, she said all three of her grown children and two of their spouses had church wounds. One of the major woundings occurred because she rightfully expected her pastor to walk the talk. It didn't happen. The pastor had proclaimed to the congregation that he was "in" for the long haul, but after the building program began, he abruptly left. It created a deep sense of betrayal, because as she wrote, "We didn't understand why things were changed after the pastor said it wouldn't change."

Abrupt changes can produce misunderstanding. If words can be misconstrued, they often will be. The enemy of our soul will make sure of it. (2Corinthians 2:11)

## HEAVYWEIGHT SQUABBLE

The book of Acts recounts a heavyweight squabble between two titans of the faith. Paul and Barnabas had a serious misunderstanding that caused them to part company for a season. Paul, the author of much of the New Testament, and Barnabas, known as the "Son of Encouragement," had worked together for years planting many churches.

On one occasion, they were unable to reach agreement concerning a young cousin of Barnabas, John Mark. John accompanied these veteran apostles on missionary ventures (Acts 12:25, 13:5), but at one point he abruptly left the team to return to Jerusalem (Acts 13:13). Paul believed this sudden departure demonstrated unreliability in John Mark's character, disqualifying him from their "A Team."

Since Paul felt he couldn't count on John Mark, he refused to invest in him. In the Greek language he refers to the young man as "not worthy" or "not fit." We could simply dismiss Paul, known for being strong-willed, assuming that he merely overreacted. We could likewise side with Paul's decision and conclude that John Mark demonstrated an instability that barred him from this high level of ministry. Only God knows the truth. But what we must realize is that our heavenly Father can use both our overreactions and under-reactions for our good if we resolve to learn from these experiences.

Barnabas, on the other hand, had a more conciliatory personality— not prone to give up on people for past failures. As is the case in many misunderstandings, each person perceives themselves as having the "higher ground."

Concerning this incident, the original Greek language indicates Paul and Barnabas' disagreement produced an "inciting irritation." They missed understanding one another—or, you could say, they understood differently.

The book of Acts describes the event like this,

> *After some time Paul said to Barnabas, "Let's go back and visit each city where we previously preached the word of the Lord, to see how the new believers are doing." Barnabas agreed and wanted to take along John Mark. But Paul disagreed strongly, since John Mark had deserted them in Pamphylia and had not continued with them in their work. Their disagreement was so sharp that they separated. Barnabas took John Mark with him and sailed for Cyprus. (Acts 15:36–39)*

Bible commentator Adam Clarke wrote, "John Mark had been tried in trying circumstances, and he failed. Paul, therefore, would not trust him again. The affection of Barnabas led him to hope the best, and was therefore desirous to give him another trial. Barnabas would not give up: Paul would not agree."

The irony of this misunderstanding is that Paul had previously been severely misunderstood by the apostles in Jerusalem. He, being a former persecutor of Christians (Acts 7:58, 9:4, 26:10–11), was initially not trusted. "When Saul arrived in Jerusalem, he tried to meet with the believers, but they were all afraid of him. They did not believe he had truly become a believer! Then Barnabas brought him to the apostles and told them how Saul had seen the Lord on the way to Damascus and how the Lord had spoken to Saul. He also told them that Saul had preached boldly in the name of Jesus in Damascus." (Acts 9:26–27)

Now the shoe was on the other foot. Paul could extend his hand of trust to someone in question. In time, he did.

We need leaders with high standards. We equally need leaders who are gracious and compassionate, willing to forgive and overlook past shortcomings. Only the Spirit of God can help us marry the two.

Over the years, especially in my youth, I had a propensity for "foot-in-mouth" disease. One time, I was telling a congregation that the Lord would be their rear guard but inadvertently said, "The Lord's going to cover your rear." A serious moment erupted into laughter. Not what I was hoping for.

I can think back on other occasions when words I said were decidedly insensitive. Some such times made an indelible impression on me. I still have mental snapshots of facial expressions of those who heard my uninspired words. These painful memories fuel a deep conviction: "I never want to say that again!"

### RELATIONSHIP KILLERS

How many relationships have been irreparably damaged or even ended because of a misunderstanding? Misdirected passion leads to misunderstanding—premature lines drawn in the sand. Honore de Balzac, a French novelist said, "They ended as all great passions do end—by a misunderstanding."

Nearly one in five *Church Wound Survey* respondents said their wounding involved misunderstandings. But, in God, all is not lost. One woman hurt by church leaders wrote how she eventually experienced, "total forgiveness towards the ones who hurt me with their words and actions. I realized I forgave them when I found compassion in my heart for them—hard to explain this phenomenon…it may be Jesus who did this."

Our ability to forgive directly parallels our understanding of how much we have been forgiven. "Forgive as quickly and completely as the Master forgave you." (Colossians 3:13, The Message) There have been many occasions with those close to me, and even with mere acquaintances, where asking forgiveness brought about an unexpected healing that far transcended the particular offense.

We can cling to our misunderstanding, or as Jesus so flawlessly modeled, seek the greater good by seeing an offender from God's perspective. Only then can we regain the true value of every wound we have received. As God redeemed us, so we can recover all that was lost. That has always been God's plan for His fallen creation.

John Newton, a former slave ship captain, painfully wrote this song after being forgiven for the genocide of 20,000 slaves: "Amazing Grace, how sweet the sound, that saved a wretch like me. I once was lost but now am found, was blind, but now I see."

We have all spoken words that became daggers in the hearts of others.

We have all misunderstood God's heart. Yet, we can now be completely forgiven.

Follow the admonition of scripture, "Let everything you say be good and helpful, so that your words will be an encouragement to those who hear them." (Ephesians 4:29b)

"I learned to forgive fast," one survey respondent wrote. "I really struggled with that in the past. I would hold grudges and justify my pain. Forgiveness frees. I can say that I can forgive and forget now with great ease. This forgiveness thing alone totally transformed my life!"

Make the devil pay for his treachery. Allow the God of healing to restore your wounded soul. Jesus, who suffered more than we can comprehend, can heal us completely.

You can tell how much love is in a man's heart by his commitment to understand someone else. God has always been willing to understand us, even at our lowest points. We should, therefore, be willing to overlook words that failed to communicate—to turn the other cheek when slapped by thoughtlessness. Only then can we represent the God who is misunderstood every day and yet never retaliates. May this expression become a daily part of our healed vocabulary, "Sorry I missed understanding you. Let's try again."

# OFFENSES

CHAPTER SIX: *Francis Anfuso*

It is considered the greatest speech given by the most admired president in American history. The date was March 4, 1865, just 41 days prior to his tragic assassination. Having been elected to a second term, President Abraham Lincoln gave his inaugural address with skillful precision to the troubled nation. He communicated God's compassion for a wounded and divided country, ravaged by war, bleeding from the heart, mind, and body.

Lincoln summed up the delicate challenge of reuniting two polar peoples, each believing they were right, and each hoping to be vindicated by a righteous God. Empathizing with and addressing the sincerity of both the North and South, here is a segment of Lincoln's famous speech in which he addresses the paradox of prayer:

> *Both read the same Bible and pray to the same God, and each invokes His aid against the other. It may seem strange that any men should dare to ask a just God's assistance in wringing their bread from the sweat of other men's faces, but let us judge not, that we be not judged. The prayers of both could not be answered. That of neither has been answered fully.*

> *The Almighty has His own purposes. "Woe unto the world because of offenses; for it must needs be that offenses come, but woe to that man by whom the offense cometh." If we shall suppose that American slavery is one of those offenses which, in the providence of God, must needs come, but which, having continued through His appointed time, He now wills to remove.*

The topic of offense covers an array of issues scaling from slight to serious. Some aspects can even reach the level of scandal, as was the case of forced slavery that Lincoln addressed. This was a heinous indignity and offended both God and man. Other relational wounds, though significant, offend on a smaller scale. But all offenses hurt and everyone gets offended. As Jesus confided, "It is impossible that no offenses should come, but woe to him through whom they do come!" (Luke 17:1b, NKJV)

Nearly one in four of those who took the *Church Wounds Survey* said they carried offenses from their involvement in church. If we aspire to be God's agents, administering His justice to a fallen world, then we must have His gracious heart to heal and "not be overcome by evil, but overcome evil with good." (Romans 12:21)

Jesus warned against intentionally stumbling others when He cautioned, "Woe to the world because of offenses! For offenses must come, but woe to that man by whom the offense comes!" (Matthew 18:7, NKJV) The word "offense" in the Greek is *skandalon* from which is derived the word "scandal," which speaks of stumbling blocks, traps or impediments. Church wounds have perpetrated many a scandal.

As President Lincoln stated so well, we must do all we can to rub healing salve into the wounds of those we have offended, not hurtful salt. All will not appreciate our efforts, as is painfully evident in our fallen President's assassination. But, there is a God in Heaven who sees in secret and rewards openly. (Matthew 6:18)

### LOVE COVERS

Too many times in my Christian life I have seen people who meant well but offended others with thoughtless words or careless actions. Yet, God's heart is always to heal through conviction, never to harm by condemnation. "God did not send His Son into the world to condemn it, but to save it." (John 3:17) If saving what was lost is truly why Jesus came into the world, then we must model this as well.

Why do we enter any room—any conversation: to heal or to hurt; to console or to condemn? The answer to this question will determine who we represent.

"He who covers over an offense promotes love, but whoever repeats the matter separates close friends." (Proverbs 17:9, NIV) Have we come to promote the angry details of our victimization or grace-filled response that shows sincere onlookers God's heart? The only way to be healed is to have a healthy attitude toward God and others, a healthy response to the setbacks of life and a healthy perspective that reflects God's purpose more than our pain. Let us mirror the God of peace who settles all accounts with intentional love.

We will eventually misrepresent God if we see Him primarily as a dogmatic Judge and not a tenderhearted Father. We may imagine God forcing His creation into subjection rather than wooing it into a love relationship. Remember, however, He chose to come to Earth in the person of God the Son, Jesus. "For the Son of Man has come to seek and to save that which was lost." (Luke 19:10) He didn't come to, "search and destroy all of His rebellious subjects."

What do we seek from those who have hurt us: retribution or reconciliation? Our motive will determine our message. Jesus affirmed this when He said, "For out of the abundance of the heart the mouth speaks." (Matthew 12:34b, NRSV)

We will never be able to reflect God's heart until we clearly see it.

King David sinned against God by committing adultery and murder. He had sent one of His most loyal subjects, Uriah, to die in a battle he couldn't win. This was after David had seduced Uriah's wife and tried to cover his sin with lies. Then the prophet Nathan came to tell David what God thought of the entire matter. His shocking words uncover the true intent of God's heart for all of us.

*The Lord, the God of Israel, says: I anointed you king of Israel and saved you from the power of Saul. I gave you your master's house and his wives and the kingdoms of Israel and Judah. And if that had not been enough, I would have given you much, much more. (2Samuel 12:7b–8)*

What a heart!

God did not say through the prophet, "I wish I'd never created you! I wish I'd never blessed you!" Or, "In retrospect, I should have given you so much less." Nathan came with the exact opposite message, a true word from the heart of God that we each so desperately need to hear today: "My heart, my son, was never to deprive you. For truly I would have given you whatever you needed."

Who can resist this kind of love?

Who would refuse to follow a leader like this?

Every aspect of God's heart is willing to forgive, to withhold nothing for our good. He truly is a generous God! If we are to genuinely represent Him, then we must do no less...speak no less.

We are not here to cast blame, but rather to live blameless lives. As Paul expressed this deepest of all concerns, "We give no offense in anything, that our ministry may not be blamed." (2Corinthians 6:3, NKJV) The original language literally means we don't want to "do anything which causes others to stumble." Another translation expresses it this way, "we put no stumbling-block in anyone's path, so that our ministry will not be discredited." (2Corinthians 6:3, NIV) As we can say and do things that stumble and lead people away from Jesus, we can likewise demonstrate that we truly know God by our genuine love in word and deed.

## HEALING OFFENSES

One mature woman wrote in our *Church Wounds Survey*, "There is great danger in courting the 'spirit' of offense. It is a sin and allows Satan a foothold into one's life. When we receive wounds we should take them immediately to the Lord; we should not talk about them unless necessary with the parties involved. We must realize that the Church is Christ's Body whom He loves."

What should we do when offenses come?

The Bible clearly sums up the proper protocols for restoration. Jesus Himself provided the divine equation, "If another believer sins against you, go privately and point out the fault. If the other person listens and confesses it, you have won that person back. But if you are unsuccessful, take one or two others with you and go back again, so that everything you say may be confirmed by two or three witnesses." (Matthew 18:15–16)

At times, this Matthew 18 sequence resolves the breach, but as one *Church Wounds Survey* participant wisely surmised, "Forgiveness is a decision. Reconciliation is a life-long process."

The vital qualities needed to successfully bring closure to offense are found in a healed heart. Paul describes them in detail: "Clothe yourselves with tenderhearted mercy, kindness, humility, gentleness, and patience. You must make allowance for each other's faults and forgive the person who offends you. Remember, the Lord forgave you, so you must forgive others." (Colossians 3:12b–13) A worthy incentive for forgiving others is being forgiven ourselves.

One of the more profound statements in the survey came from a man who had lived long and learned a lot. He wrote, "Wounding is part of life in a fallen world. To expect anything else is naive. Jesus knew men. Get through the confusion they cause quickly, with grace and forgiveness, knowing that we wound each other all the time, without intention. Dwell on the good and pray for its increase. God will take care of the causes of offense and missed expectations in His time."

President Lincoln's efforts to facilitate reconciliation proved unsuccessful during his lifetime, even leading to his death. It would take generations for complete healing. Nevertheless, because of his pursuit of peace, our nation would eventually unite and thrive again.

> *"With malice toward none, with charity for all, with firmness in the right as God gives us to see the right, let us strive on to finish the work we are in, to bind up the nation's wounds, to care for him who shall have borne the battle and for his widow and his orphan, to do all which may achieve and cherish a just and lasting peace among ourselves and with all nations."*

This conclusion to Lincoln's second inaugural address emphasizes that whether or not others receive our efforts to defuse offenses, we are still called to "Pursue peace with all people, and holiness, without which no one will see the Lord." (Hebrews 12:14) We will not see God move or heal, nor will we understand God's intent unless we follow the road to peace, ever careful not to compromise genuine holiness. Peace without holiness leads to appeasement without principle. True peace will never conflict with the truth of God's Word.

Jesus promised a great reward for those willing to disarm offenses. "Blessed are the peacemakers, for they shall be called sons of God." (Matthew 5:9, NKJV) What matters most is not what man calls us, but fulfilling the call of God on our lives. Be a peacemaker and you will authentically represent the Prince of Peace. (Isaiah 9:6)

# HYPOCRISY

Section Three

# PROMISES UNFULFILLED

## CHAPTER SEVEN: *Francis Anfuso*

*There is no greater fraud than a promise not kept.*—Gaelic Proverb

A couple of years ago, I was playing golf with a friend named Danny when he received a phone call that his stepfather had lost his fight with cancer. We immediately stopped our game and, while driving away, Danny told me this story.

His step-dad was the only man in his childhood he believed in. The abandonment and neglect of his biological father had left Danny completely untrusting of men. It would take his step-dad many painstaking years to overcome the hurts his bio-dad had inflicted.

One of these hurts happened when he promised to take Danny golfing. He adored and missed his father as a young boy, especially after his parents divorced. This made time with dad even more desirable. One day, his dad called promising to take Danny golfing. The moment he hung up the phone Danny ran to the garage to retrieve his clubs. He then spent what seemed like the rest of the night shining each club, one by one. When he finished, Danny set them by the front door so he wouldn't delay his dad once he arrived.

The next morning the 10-year old waited for his dad, but he never showed up, called, or ever apologized to his son for his broken promise. Danny was devastated. It made an indelible wound on his fragile soul. Now, with the death of his step-dad, the only loving father he had ever known, Danny put in perspective the depth of his loss by comparing him to his natural father.

Thirty years later, you could still feel the raw emotion of that one unfulfilled promise in the heart of a child. I will never forget his tear-filled eyes as he recounted the story.

What captures our imagination more than a promise?

What crushes our hopes more than a promise broken?

Broken promises overwhelm us with disappointment. Hitting the ground with disintegrating force, the breach of trust leaves us bewildered and broken-hearted. Perhaps nothing that happens in life jolts us to our core quite as much as a promise unfulfilled.

## THE POWER OF A PROMISE

Ah, springtime! Anticipation of something extraordinary is awakened. In spring, new life is everywhere. Flowers bloom with the fragrance of new beginnings.

A promise is much like springtime. We believe again, letting down our guard to await a return on our dreams. We have each seen fruit that delights our senses. We have each tasted the blessed hope we so desperately long for.

Each of us is blessed when we see the first buds of promise begin to bloom. But a dying dream cuts to the very core of our being. The unthinkable has happened. Divorce…bankruptcy…disease…unfaithfulness… adultery…dishonesty, they each gouge our heart and leave us lying listless.

No promise is needed for the mundane. It must be exceptional in order to merit a level of commitment called a *promise*. At times, in order for us to buy in at this highest level of allegiance, a promise is needed; a vow is required; an oath must be made. The event is so special, people are invited to the ceremony: a marriage, a dedication, a baptism, or a grand opening. Champagne hits the hull and we are off and running.

When, on occasion, we realize our dream cruise is aboard the Titanic, our hopes plummet to the bottom of the sea.

Some of us know people who have celebrated 50 years or more of marriage. The devotion of these couples is often so rare it evokes thunderous applause.

In the business community, well-established companies print the founding year in their advertising to let people know, "We've been around for a while!" "We've weathered storms and will be here for you." "You can count on us!" "We will keep our promises!"

This is partly why the ministry for men, *Promise Keepers*, was so life changing. In an age of broken commitments and shattered covenants, men rose up to fight to fulfill their vows, invoking a springtime of hope to the barren landscape of infidelity and divorce. Wives were elated to send their husbands. I know mine was. "Go get 'em honey! Come back a renewed man, ready to keep the oath you made to me and our children!"

I left commissioned and returned resolute.

On our wedding day way back in 1975, I knew well the instability of my relational commitments prior to becoming a Christian. Chronic unfaithfulness, coupled with the solemnity of my marriage vows, inspired me to write and sing a song to my beautiful wife, Suzie, on our wedding day. The chorus proclaimed: "Suzie I won't fail you, have no fear. No, Suzie I won't fail you, until our Lord He does appear." I sang to my life-partner with a slight level of trepidation. Now, decades later, I am humbled and blessed beyond measure to have been able to fulfill this pledge to the bride of my youth.

## NUMB AND NUMBER

Broken promises are the open wound hindering the next generation from making commitments. The upshot of this chronic unfaithfulness, modeled by parents and leaders, has left masses emotionally numb to the very concept of making vows and promises of any kind.

They'll cohabitate, but will not marry.

Visit, but do not commit.

Experience, but will not fully surrender.

In the end, restrained love isn't love at all. It is conditional and muted by fear and uncertainty. A calloused heart remains unable to feel as God intended.

The Bible says, "Hope deferred makes the heart sick, but when dreams come true, there is life and joy." (Proverbs 13:12) How many, crushed by disappointment, have lost hope that dreams or promises will ever be fulfilled? Languished with shattered hearts, the faithfulness they long for stays out of reach, unless their hearts are healed and their hope is restored.

Such is the experience of millions who imagined the best, but experienced the beast. Words once dreamed of, "for better, for worse; for richer, for poorer; in sickness and in health, 'til death do us part," now serve as haunting reminders of what will never be. Crushed under the weight of irreconcilable differences, past assurances are now daggers to the heart, remnants of a shattered bond.

The distrust in broken church relationships can replicate the pain suffered in a shattered marriage. Once the honeymoon was over, so was the commitment.

Dropped again.

Left hanging.

We hoped. We believed. We trusted.

In the end, we were devastated.

In many cases, this was not the beginning of sorrows, it was the sequel.

Children often replicate the life-altering ritual of promises broken. Kind will beget kind, until at some miraculous future moment the cycle of pain is broken. If it is not, then these vulnerable ones will enter a church environment, prime candidates for further wounding.

Expectations will be dashed...misunderstandings will occur...offenses will come.

Either we conquer the battle of past poor responses, or we will be jolted yet again with "the left-hook from hell."

Nearly one in four *Church Wounds Survey* responders said they were hurt because of promises unfulfilled. One older man wrote: "Leaders set promises and implications before people that didn't materialize." adding, "It's easy for leaders to mistake their personal ministries for 'church.' Everyone becomes part of his or her personal mission, which may be mistaken with God's mission."

Whether on a grand, church-wide level, or in the course of daily interpersonal relationships, promises made and commitments extended, may be yanked at the most unsuspecting moment.

## PRESUMPTUOUS PROMISES

Rarely do people make promises intending to break them. At a moment of unbridled inspiration, we launch a hope-filled sentence, pledge a lofty goal, sign a legal document, or make an enthusiastic commitment that others view as an opportunity to hang their dreams on. "I'll be there for you!" "We'll do it together." Like buying into an investment when expectations are high, we never anticipate the crash. Yet, the unthinkable does, on occasion, show up and plans are either changed or completely dismantled.

When it comes to speculative future events, we must be careful to not attach people's hopes to our capacity to fulfill them. "Unless the LORD builds the house, they labor in vain who build it; unless the LORD guards the city, the watchman keeps awake in vain." (Psalm 127:1) God is the ultimate finisher, yet He will only commit to finish what He alone authors. We cannot send God the bill for our presumptions.

James, the brother of Jesus cautions, "Come now, you who say, 'Today or tomorrow we will go to such and such a city, spend a year there, buy and sell, and make a profit'; whereas you do not know what will happen tomorrow. For what is your life? It is even a vapor that appears for a little time and then vanishes away. Instead you ought to say, 'If the Lord wills, we shall live and do this or that.' But now you boast in your arrogance. All such boasting is evil." (James 4:13–17, NKJV)

If our promise to others is birthed out of pride or arrogance, it is sin, and will only bring a harvest of pain. *Any* promise we make and do not fulfill can stumble one of God's precious ones, bringing reproach to Jesus' name. Forgiveness must be asked and, if needed, restitution should be made.

### PROMISES FULFILLED

God never intended promises to be the saboteur of relationships! In fact, promises and covenants are meant to enhance and protect relationships. The *Great Promise Maker* is also the *Eternal Promise Keeper*. "God is not a man, that He should lie. He is not a human, that He should change His mind. Has He ever spoken and failed to act? Has He ever promised and not carried through?" (Numbers 23:19) The answer to these rhetorical questions is a resounding, "Never!" God is the personification of faithfulness. "[He] has said, 'Never will I leave you; never will I forsake you.' (Hebrews 13:5b, NIV)

The flawless faithfulness of God is that sure tower that stands ever ready to shelter us. "Praise the LORD who has given rest to His people Israel, just as He promised. Not one word has failed of all the wonderful promises He gave through His servant Moses." (1Kings 8:56)

God cannot fail, and He won't fail you!

We are able to fully rest in the faithful arms of Jesus when we are persuaded He truly is the *Great Promise Keeper*. He is the One who pledges and fulfills, who starts and finishes. He never leaves us hanging—abandoned and heart-broken. Frankly, we do it to ourselves.

A seasoned Christian, bruised by many church wounds, which included unfulfilled financial promises, wrote in his survey: "My church wounds are overshadowed by the wounds of Jesus! The Lord does not waste any wound. He uses ALL to reach others with His love and grace."

Though a natural reaction to such a wounding would be anger, this man chose two supernatural responses instead. First, he disciplined his soul to focus on the sufferings of Jesus, realizing His Savior had suffered far more than he.

Secondly, over time, the Lord revealed the true value of all the pain this man had been through. It prepared him as a vessel capable of loving and caring for others. God was then able to use this humbled man to model the grace that is available to all who truly trust in Him.

Though this Christian's extraordinary perspective provides a simple and concise description of how to pristinely respond to the greatest offenses in life, it requires both the miracles of faith and forgiveness in order to arrive at such a wise and generous place.

When the patriarch Joseph lay in prison, the victim of yet another injustice, a divine opportunity presented itself. He made an appeal to someone capable of ending his plight, Pharaoh's chief butler. Like Joseph, the butler had fallen upon hard times and had been imprisoned himself.

Joseph interpreted the butler's dream that described how Pharaoh would soon free him. When the dream came true, and the butler was about to be released, Joseph entreated him to intercede on his behalf before Pharaoh. The butler said he would, but forgot. (Genesis 39 and 40)

Two long years went by. Joseph's focus became guarding his heart from becoming bitter. (Proverbs 4:23) He didn't want an unfulfilled promise to become a stumbling block, keeping him bound in the disgruntled world of disappointment. Instead, he purposed to view it as a stepping-stone, taking him deeper into the will and purpose of God.

Each of us has the same choice today.

May we arrive sooner than later at the mature place of rest and trust what our father Abraham found so comforting, "Abraham never wavered in believing God's promise. In fact, his faith grew stronger, and in this he brought glory to God. He was absolutely convinced that God was able to do anything He promised." (Romans 4:20–21)

In the end, there are only two kinds of people inhabiting this troubled planet. Some live as mere victims of the unfaithfulness of others. And some, who view life from God's perspective, can grow to become people who learn, through much pain and struggle, to trust the One whose promises never fail.

The choice is ours to make.

Choose wisely.

# HYPOCRISY

## CHAPTER EIGHT: *David Loveless*

While in college, I encouraged many high school kids to give their lives to Christ. That was during the raw, wild days of the Jesus Movement when I wore bell-bottoms and a headband and told everyone to, "Just keep it real, man!" I experienced significant spiritual growth until blatant lack of authenticity in a group of church leaders sabotaged my passion.

These leaders sang in the choir, chaired committees, prayed publicly, and sometimes led the services. They met monthly in closed sessions to discuss the direction of the church, berating the pastor and various aspects of his leadership. Their poor church behavior was nothing compared to how they lived at home. I know because their kids were my good friends.

One leader, I'll call Dan, had weekly patterns of drunkenness, rage, physical abuse, and profane language. His wife and kids lived in constant fear of what he would do next. Then Sunday came and Dan put on his coat and tie ready to play the part of a good Christian leader.

Nothing I ever saw in Dan demonstrated that his beliefs impacted his behavior.

Sadly, it was the Christ-less character of Dan and his friends that the enemy used to distract me from the real issues in my own soul. I didn't know it at the time, but I used their two-faced living as an excuse to abandon my commitment to a Christ-centered life. I spent my freshmen and sophomore years engulfed in psychological and philosophical theory. To anyone who would listen, I declared the Church a sham.

Just about everyone has uttered these words, heard these words, or thought these infamous words: "the Church is full of hypocrites." Countless people have been faith-wrecked, tossing the Church to the curb because of this belief.

So really—what is a hypocrite? It is a person who pretends to have virtues, beliefs, or standards that they don't actually possess. The actual word "hypocrisy" comes from the Greek language referring to "play-acting" or "acting out." Its literal meaning refers to playing a part, giving a performance or hearing dramatic text by an actor involving a large degree of interpretation.

Jesus had a lot to say about religious actors pretending to be kingdom players.

> *So when you give to the needy, do not announce it with trumpets, as the hypocrites do in the synagogues and on the streets, to be honored by men. I tell you the truth; they have received their reward in full. But when you give to the needy, do not let your left hand know what your right hand is doing, so that your giving may be in secret. Then your Father, who sees what is done in secret, will reward you. And when you pray, do not be like the hypocrites, for they love to pray standing in the synagogues and on the street corners to be seen by men. I tell you the truth, they have received their reward in full…When you fast, do not look somber as the hypocrites do, for they disfigure their faces to show men they are fasting. I tell you the truth, they have received their reward in full. (Matthew 6: 2–5,16)*

### NIGHTMARE ON CHURCH STREET

It hurts to discover esteemed people playing a part instead of living the part. It confuses. It royally trips us up.

Some time ago, a pastor in a neighboring city sent the spiritual destinies of a whole host of Christ-followers sprawling to the pavement. The pastor led one of the most well-known churches in the country. Through his teaching and leadership, God brought a spiritual awakening of significant renown. Later, it was discovered he had been acting a part. For a number of years he had been immorally involved with a number of women.

News of this nightmare hit like an end-time earthquake. Local and national periodicals exposed the man and defamed his church. People were beyond stunned. Not *this* guy! Not *our* pastor! The way he taught, the examples he used made it appear as if he was living all he believed. Scores abandoned the standing-room-only sanctuary. The pastor resigned in shame. He could not go home. He had no job. Only half a handful of friends would even speak to him. For several years, stories poured from multitudes who felt nothing the pastor taught could be trusted. A great church with a wide, bright light was suddenly snuffed out.

Was this pastor wrong? Clearly.

Did he devastate thousands of Christians and jade hundreds of thousands of others to the claims of Christ? Clearly.

Was he a hypocrite? Yes, he was. He portrayed one kind of life when he, in fact, lived another.

Did the pastor, who diligently taught truths from God's Word, negate its truth by his sin? Let's think about that for a moment.

What if you went to your doctor for a physical and in the course of that exam he chastised you for your smoking habit and listed all of its risks? Then after you left his office and were seated in your car you notice him lighting a cigarette? What would you think? Would you want to jump from your car and yell, "hypocrite?" Probably. But was he wrong to advise you that smoking is dangerous? No. His advice was still correct.

A doctor who smokes (and there are plenty of them) is a hypocrite for advising one thing and living another. But, the fact that he or she smokes does not negate the truth shared. Should we dismiss flawless advice from a flawed messenger? I think not, especially if the truth of the message can set us free.

## TAKES ONE TO KNOW ONE

Most of us are guilty (I know I am) of calling groups or individuals on things they aren't living up to while failing to face our own hypocrisies.

Again, Jesus seemed to burn a lot of energy around this subject. "The Pharisee stood up and prayed about himself: 'God, I thank you that I am not like other men—robbers, evildoers, adulterers—or even like this tax collector.'" (Luke 18:11) Jesus retorted, "You hypocrite, first take the plank out of your own eye, and then you will see clearly to remove the speck from your brother's eye." (Matthew 7:5)

It is often easier for me to identify the inconsistencies in someone else's life than to face my own. Jesus seems to be saying, when irritation over someone's failure creeps in, first go to the mirror and measure which side of my mouth is speaking.

The real, sad fact of life is this: none of us live up to all the truth we know and believe. All of us have a sizable gap between the standards we set for ourselves and how we actually live. There is hypocrisy in all of us.

You may have heard the statement, "When you point one finger at me, you have four pointing back at you!"

One of the men who took our survey acknowledged this when he wrote, "I finally left my last church as the result of what I considered to be hypocrisy on the part of the senior minister and other church leaders. What they said and did were seldom the same. After leaving, I realized I was just as much a hypocrite as they were but did not know at the time how to recover."

How should we view those who appear to be examples?

All of us need parents. We need guides. We need leaders. We seek to learn new things and go to new places in the kingdom of God. Most often we count on someone who is more experienced to show us the way; someone who we hope has our best interest in mind.

"One of you says, 'I follow Paul;' another, 'I follow Apollos;' another, 'I follow Cephas;' still another, 'I follow Christ.'" (1Corinthians 1:12) The apostle Paul was a guide. He was a spiritual parent. He was definitely a godly leader. He knew that, by the grace of God, there was enough consistency in his life to admonish others to follow him. However, Paul never claimed to be a flawless truth carrier.

Ponder these scriptures for a moment, realizing they came from the same first century leader after whom many of us admire and model our lives and ministries.

> *Follow my example as I follow the example of Christ. (1Corinthians 11:1)*

> *I do not understand what I do. For what I want to do I do not do, but what I hate I do… I know that nothing good lives in me, that is, in my sinful nature. For I have the desire to do what is good, but I cannot carry it out. For what I do is not the good I want to do; no, the evil I do not want to do—this I keep on doing. Now if I do what I do not want to do, it is no longer I who do it, but it is sin living in me that does it. (Romans 7:15–20)*

The same apostle who said "follow my example" is the same one who confessed, throughout Romans 6–7 that he couldn't seem to get himself to consistently attain what he believed and wanted to do. And yet, we allow this person to act as a major spiritual father for our lives.

I wonder if there were people who felt Paul was a hypocrite.

Jesus modeled the true Christian life in the context of discipleship. He was the last perfect mentor on Earth. Since then, the best we can hope to follow are sons of men, not the Son of Man, keeping both eyes on Jesus as we learn from His under-shepherds.

But what about those in the church that knowingly and consistently act as hypocrites and do nothing to address the hurt they cause? The Bible has some very specific instruction.

*If your brother sins against you go and show him his fault, just between the two of you. If he listens to you, you have won your brother over. But if he will not listen, take one or two others along, so that every matter may be established by the testimony of two or three witnesses. If he refuses to listen to them, tell it to the church; and if he refuses to listen even to the church, treat him as you would a pagan or a tax collector. (Matthew 18:15–17)*

### HEALING THE WOUNDS OF HYPOCRISY

- Realize that every person you meet who claims to be a Christ-follower or leader is a person who first and foremost is a pilgrim. He is still in the middle of his own journey and has not arrived at the final destination. He is going to sin and make mistakes. Prepare to forgive him.

- Understand you will feel more mercy and grace for others when you square up with your own shortcomings. Ask God to keep your own heart filled with compassion.

- Remember, the truth has not been negated even though it was taught or modeled by a follower who violates one or more of its principles. The truth you were taught is still valid. "The Word of God does not return void." (Isaiah 55:11)

- Ask God to mend what less-than-authentic leaders crushed. Ask Him to help you see through His grace-filled, untainted eyes.

- Ask God to bring correction to those who appear to be hypocrites. Ask Him to be as merciful as possible in His discipline with them, as merciful as you would want Him to be with you. "For there will be no mercy for you if you have not been merciful to others." (James 2:13a)

I made a rookie mistake the first time I went snow skiing. I opted for no lessons. After all how hard could it be? Before the trip, to save cash, I checked out an instruction manual from the library and practiced snow-plow techniques on our living room rug. Piece of cake, I thought.

Right.

I spent my entire first day insanely sliding and crashing down one giant mountain in Snowmass, Colorado. You could *technically* say I was a skier but nothing I did resembled the familiar zigzag tracks of Wide-World-of-Sports skiers. Oh, there was no thrill of victory, only the agony of defeat. Still, I gave the experience every ounce of knowledge I had. I dressed the part, read the book, but at best I was a clownish imitation of an ideal alpine athlete. If you had seen me that day you might have said, "David is a hypocrite. And he calls himself a skier. What a joke."

I must have looked a lot like those church leaders from my teen years whose behavior so fried my faith. We both had a long way to grow. Since that time, I hope I have gained more perspective on myself and those around me. My church wounds from hypocrisy have healed and I have completely released those leaders and others whom the enemy hoped I would keep in an emotional prison.

I want to leave you with one of the most significant statements ever made. I hope you will keep it in mind whenever you are tempted to judge hypocrites that come across your path. We can only ever control the lives we lead before others. So, whatever happens, "Just keep it real, man!"

# MISREPRESENTATION

## CHAPTER NINE: *Francis Anfuso*

*"Rather fail with honor than succeed by fraud."*—Sophocles

They loved as brothers, facing the ridicule of the religious leaders as one. For years they traveled inseparably, sharing finances, food, and friendship. A relationship so close, absolute trust extended into every dimension without ever a question of loyalty.

Therefore, on the night of the double-cross, no one saw it coming. Above suspicion, the dependable friend was the last person anyone suspected. Yet, this once close comrade perpetrated the greatest sellout in history. The cruelest of crimes left him branded as one of the most contemptible figures of all time. Even today, his name brings a shudder.

Just hours after the betrayal, he was dead by his own hand. What atrocious behavior could cause such swift judgment? What evil act could incite some to say, "It would be better for him if he had never been born?" (Matthew 26:24) What diabolical deception could entice one so steadfast to sabotage his future?

It was not just the cruelty of the crime that still shocks us thousands of years after its premeditation, but how it was evil cloaked in virtue. The traitor adorned his despicable act with love and kindness, masquerading deceit and cunning in the most tender of gestures.

Only those closest to us, have the capacity to hurt us most. What could wound more than stabbing someone in the back during an endearing embrace?

A duplicitous act—thought to be the epitome of affection and care—was disguised in a lie. The kiss of death made him one of the most disdained persons who ever lived, his name untouchable for generations.

Judas!

Would anyone in his or her right mind consider naming a son Judas? I think not!

Judas' misrepresentation of love and friendship left an unforgivable wound. Jesus acknowledged the self-destruction of his disciple, Judas. "None has been lost except the one doomed to destruction so that Scripture would be fulfilled." (John 17:12, NIV)

A misrepresentation of love doomed the fabricator to hell.

From a legal perspective, misrepresentation is called *fraud*. Defined as, "a person or thing intended to deceive others, typically by unjustifiably claiming or being credited with accomplishments or qualities."[7] Fraud's intent is always to deceive. The father of lies pre-meditates deceit. As Jesus told the Jewish authorities in Jerusalem, "For you are the children of your father the Devil, and you love to do the evil things he does. He was a murderer from the beginning and has always hated the truth. There is no truth in him. When he lies, it is consistent with his character; for he is a liar and the father of lies." (John 8:44)

Who is our father?

Whose character do we resemble?

The Father of Light, dispelling all darkness with truth, or the father of lies, cowering in the shadows of misrepresentation and deceit?

*Deceit*, defined as "the action or practice of deceiving someone by concealing or misrepresenting the truth,"[8] is birthed in hell. Its effects are so ruinous that they seem unredeemable. As the writer Frederick W. Robertson surmised, "There are three things in the world that deserve no mercy: hypocrisy, fraud, and tyranny."

---

7    "fraud." The Oxford Pocket Dictionary of Current English. 2009. Available at http://www.encyclopedia.com/doc/10999-fraud.html. Last accessed January 3, 2010.

8    "deceit." The Oxford Pocket Dictionary of Current English. 2009. Available at http://www.encyclopedia.com/doc/10999-deceit.html. Last accessed January 3, 2010.

If fraud is judged this harshly in the world, how much more grievous is misrepresentation when it is a cancer in the Church?

## WONDERFUL NONSENSE

When the great War to End All Wars ended, people's eyes reflected dollar signs and an unbridled willingness to break with tradition. Enter the Roaring 20s!

It was called the *Age of Wonderful Nonsense,* a decade brimming with boundless prospects, economic boom, and technological breakthroughs. The North and South Poles were explored, Mt. Everest was climbed, and women were awarded the vote. With a renaissance in nature, and the pioneering of radio, records, and movies, seemingly endless opportunities abounded.

As brightly as it began, it ended with a cataclysmic crash, sending a generation into despair.

During this decade of possibilities, a man named Charles Ponzi told thousands of would-be investors that his "mail coupons" would earn them a 40% return in just 90 days. Ponzi received over $1 million in a three-hour period. Attempting to legitimize the scam, he paid off early investors with money from new investors. Friends told friends. The fraud escalated.

In the end, an investigation determined Ponzi had spent only $30 on the mail coupons. But the con was on, and the phrase Ponzi scheme had its ignominious origin.

Since that time, others have taken this form of embezzlement to new depths. Bernard Madoff made off with over $50 billion of investors' monies in 2008. For his treachery he will spend 150 years in prison.

How many of us enter our own *Age of Wonderful Nonsense,* misrepresenting God for personal, immediate gain?

The only reason the scales of justice remain balanced between a holy God and sinful man is because Jesus bore the punishment our transgressions deserve.

Denial never brings equity. Fraud promotes further distrust, which can last for generations. This cycle can only be broken by an unabashed commitment to truth at all costs and a firm dedication to take full responsibility for every thoughtless word or deed perpetrated against others.

## VIOLATING VIRTUE

The legal maxim states, "It is fraud to conceal fraud." This is so in the spirit realm, too. To mislead God's people by misrepresenting His character, life, and Word is fraud. A spiritual Ponzi scheme capitalizes on the hopes of the naïve and vulnerable. Desperate people are lured into believing the slick assurances of charismatic charlatans.

The Bible implicitly warns against empty promises of deceivers. They lead others astray. "I have not written to you because you do not know the truth, but because you know it, and that no lie is of the truth." (1John 2:21, NKJV)

The truth frees, while lies enslave. (John 8:32) "Fraud and falsehood only dread examination," writes the 18th century author Samuel Johnson. "Truth invites it."

This is why some church wounds hurt so deeply. Dreams are awakened and aroused by seemingly miraculous possibilities only to be dashed by fraud and misrepresentation. Promised love, we anticipate unconditional acceptance. Offered a new beginning, we dive in, believing that our past hurts and regrets can at last be redeemed. Promises fulfilled bring bliss. New beginnings unfulfilled leave only heartache.

Their words offered life, but the letter of their unfulfillment delivered death. "For the letter kills, but the Spirit gives life." (2Corinthians 3:6b, NKJV)

Perhaps the greatest tragedy is that the effect of misrepresentation leaves us cynical and untrusting. We can even question the veracity of God's magnificent truths and assurances. This startling consequence strips us of hope and can even destroy our ability to become all God intended.

One thoroughly disheartened twenty-something wrote in our *Church Wounds Survey,* "Several of the people that attended my last church went to Bible studies and Sunday services, then were seen misrepresenting Christ: drinking, drugs, adultery etc. I honestly felt more attacked and unaccepted at church than by any of my friends who were promiscuous. At least they came by it honestly and didn't live with a delusional notion that they were 'saved' once a week after spiritual activities."

Later she described her present, healthy church experience as "Christ-centered, with a lot of healed people, where standards are raised to biblical standards and the gospel is not watered down to let people continue their [sinful] lifestyles." She went on to say she was impacted by, "An emphasis on prayer and forgiveness from God and between my current relationships, learning the truth of what God says about how we should really live, and having forgiveness and compassion for people who are not living it."

In another response, one heart-broken mother recounted, "Our then 16 year old son, who was a pillar in the youth group, was ill for two years, missing his junior and senior years in high school. No one from the church came to see him, even after repeated attempts asking for prayer from his youth pastor and asking the elders to come and pray for him. Nothing!" Though she and her husband have remained faithful in a healthy church since that time, their son does not walk with God. This gross oversight left a wound yet to be healed.

### FREED FROM FRAUD

The occasional misrepresentation of a flawless God by flawed people is not just likely, but guaranteed. Therefore, a pattern of humbly acknowledging our shortcomings must become second nature. Otherwise, we will call ourselves flawless, while being flawed, and misrepresent a flawless God.

A true representative of Jesus must regularly admit, "I was wrong. Would you please forgive me?" Periodically, I've asked our congregation to repeat these power-filled words reminding them that they should be the regular confession of sincere Christ-followers.

God help us! Help us to not continue the charade of distorting Your sublime Spirit.

The passionate pursuit of life or death has always been our choice. God's offer still stands after thousands of years. "Today I have given you the choice between life and death, between blessings and curses. I call on heaven and earth to witness the choice you make. Oh, that you would choose life, that you and your descendants might live!" (Deuteronomy 30:19)

We are freed from the fraud by acknowledging the fake.

We are liberated from the lie by exposing the impostor within us.

"O wretched man that I am! Who will deliver me from this body of death? I thank God—through Jesus Christ our Lord!" (Romans 7:24–25a, NKJV)

"It is absolutely clear that God has called you to a free life. Just make sure that you don't use this freedom as an excuse to do whatever you want to do and destroy your freedom. Rather, use your freedom to serve one another in love; that's how freedom grows." (Galatians 5:13, The Message)

Has your misrepresentation of Jesus Christ wounded others? Have your words or actions cheated them out of knowing truth that will set them free? (Romans 8:32) It's not too late to take responsibility for old sins— to own up to past embezzlements.

Your opportunity is now. "Today, if you will hear His voice, do not harden your hearts as in the rebellion." (Hebrews 3:15b, NKJV)

If, on the other hand, you have been damaged by misrepresentations, don't remain a victim. God will give you all you need to rise above the pain of your past. He will provide the willingness to yield, the insight to understand, the grace to forgive, and the heart to heal. But God will never overpower your will. If we choose to harbor bitterness and resentment, then we become bitter and resentful. If, however, we resist the urge to further misrepresent the heart of a kind and forgiving God, then we ourselves will represent the One whose image and likeness we bear.

We can rise above typical and become extraordinary!

The ball is now in your court. You can continue to rehearse past hurts and lick your wounds, or you can begin the journey out of past offenses and into true health. Will you forgive leaders who misled, friends who abandoned, and Christians who were less than Christ-like?

Doing right is infinitely more fulfilling than being right.

I can correct my misrepresentation.

Let it begin with me.

# HALF-TRUTHS

## CHAPTER TEN: *Francis Anfuso*

*"If you always tell the truth, you never have to remember anything."*—Mark Twain

Why is dishonesty so damaging to a leader, especially a Christian leader? Because it destroys trust! If we can't believe someone, we'll never know when he is telling the truth, even if he claims to be a follower of Jesus. The very nature of the Christian faith is absolutely dependent upon credibility—being fully persuaded that God, the Bible, and a Christian is worthy of trust. When a person's integrity is brought into question, so is his believability.

So, why would someone tell a half-truth? Why would she jeopardize an entire reputation, all the good that she represents, for one misguided sentence?

Perhaps, so that people will think of her more highly, or so they will not think less.

At times, people lie in order for something to remain hidden—so that it never sees the light of day.

When a person lies, he is terribly afraid of losing something he feels is even more valuable to him than the truth. Jesus assured us, "The good man brings good things out of the good stored up in his heart, and the evil man brings evil things out of the evil stored up in his heart. For out of the overflow of his heart his mouth speaks." (Luke 6:45, NIV)

The ultimate purpose and motive behind telling a half-truth is to bring hearers to a conclusion that is false. A half-truth contains information that may be partially accurate but is fundamentally flawed. Half-truths leave a distorted impression and a counterfeit reality.

In actuality, these statements should be called "half-lies." All half-truths contain enough deception to steal, kill, and destroy the irreplaceable: trust and confidence—even in our most cherished relationships. (John 10:10) The hearer is crushed; stripped of his relational assurance, he is left dangling by treads of disappointment and disillusionment. False comfort comes from naively believing that a statement containing a measure of truth is sufficiently believable and credible.

False teachings don't have to operate with outright lies when half-truths will do. I'm persuaded that half-truths deceive more people than complete lies. The Message paraphrase challenges us, "What this adds up to, then, is this: no more lies, no more pretense. Tell your neighbor the truth. In Christ's body we're all connected to each other, after all. When you lie to others, you end up lying to yourself." (Ephesians 4:25, The Message) So, clean house! Make a clean sweep of malice and pretense, envy and hurtful talk. (1Peter 2:1)

Though I cannot begin to fully understand the literal ramifications of one of the most challenging verses in the Bible, I am unable to dismiss Revelation which states that, "all liars," will end up eternally separated from God, "in the lake that burns with fire and sulfur." (Revelation 21:8)

## EXTREME TRUTH

Half-truths remind me of the dangers inherent in extreme sports. How many have dodged near-death bullets, only to have the tide turn one ill-fated day? Time and again, I've read of gifted athletes and adventurers who danced with death one time too many. Fans idolized their astonishing exploits, only to be crushed by the finality of their excess. They fell off a mountain, plunged from the sky, took one final flip, each time believing a lie cloaked in half-truth: that they were capable of one more stunt—one more feat. They weren't. The unforgiving end came without warning, and without mercy.

A law of nature won, sealing once and for all their unsuspecting fate.

So, too, when we stretch the truth!

Instead of bending with us, it breaks us.

When we elaborate a story, overstate facts, or embellish an act of God, we grieve the Holy Spirit. Stretching the truth by exaggeration, or worse yet, using words that distort reality, invite a lethal shell game. There is a line that, when crossed, brings destruction. "Do not be deceived [led astray from the right way], God is not mocked; for whatever a man sows, that he will also reap." (Galatians 6:7, NKJV)

While some statements are flawed attempts at lessening the blow of brutal honesty, half-truths are mere cover-ups of outright lies. A Yiddish proverb says it well, "A half-truth is a whole lie."

Until we believe beyond a shadow of doubt that truth is infinitely more beautiful than lies, we'll lie when we think we have to; unwilling to swallow the truth, we end up eating lies.

What is most sad is that we have to know the truth in order to speak a lie. We trade the priceless for the worthless, pawn respect and honor for shame and disgrace. The irony of fearing that people might think less of us if they knew the truth, is that invariably they think far less of those who perpetuate a lie than those who tell the truth.

### TRUTH TELLERS

Some people are more concerned that they have been lied to than that a lie has been told. Friedrich Nietzsche said, "I'm not upset that you lied to me, I'm upset that from now on I can't believe you."

Others see little problem in telling lies, or even using them for diabolical ends. Adolf Hitler quipped, "Make the lie big, make it simple; keep saying it, and eventually they will believe it."

Perhaps nothing reveals the character of a person more than the reason for speaking a lie. But even a tiny lie can destroy a giant reputation. "The one who tells the truth will endure forever, but the one who lies will last only for a moment." (Proverbs 12:19, NET)

Mother Teresa wisely stated, "Be faithful in small things because it is in them that your strength lies." Proverbs 11:3 says, "The righteousness of the upright will be their guide, but the twisted ways of the false will be their destruction." (BBE)

Ironically, a lie need not be spoken because some lies are lived. They hurt others just as much. More people lie with silence than they do with words. When we are timid to speak the truth, lies win. When we are afraid to stand up for right, we will inevitably bow to wrong. Newspaper columnist Ann Landers wisely wrote, "The naked truth is always better than the best dressed lie."

Make no mistake about it: all lies are birthed in hell. Jesus knew it well. "The devil… has always hated the truth… there is no truth in him. When he lies, it is consistent with his character; for he is a liar and the father of lies." (John 8:44)

## SWALLOW YOUR PRIDE AND EAT YOUR WORDS

On a few occasions while speaking, I was convicted by the Holy Spirit as I communicated an inaccuracy. I then acknowledged my overstatement and restated the sentence I felt I had exaggerated earlier in the message. It was always a bit awkward, but admitting it released the presence of God in a humbling, authentic way.

Whether we like it or not, the greater our influence is, the greater the scrutiny of our credibility will be. Boast a great thing and you will be held to a higher standard. Claim to represent the God of the Universe and, though you are not perfect, you will be expected to represent Him authentically.

When I expose a lie in front of others, it does not guarantee I will never lie again. On the other hand, people know I cherish the truth. They can see me personally and aggressively unmasking a falsehood and understand this is a holy habit and not a freak accident.

Dishonest people stumble over lies, while truth-bearers look for opportunities to turn themselves in. The level of grief over a misrepresentation is an indicator of true character. "Don't grieve God. Don't break His heart. His

Holy Spirit, moving and breathing in you, is the most intimate part of your life, making you fit for Himself. Don't take such a gift for granted." (Ephesians 4:30, The Message)

If we never fight for truth, we will eventually bow to lies. Scripture challenges each of us, "No, O people, the Lord has told you what is good, and this is what He requires of you: to do what is right, to love mercy, and to walk humbly with your God." (Micah 6:8)

My eagerness, not just willingness, to eat humble pie, speaks of the side I choose: the God who is Truth (John 14:6), not the devil who deceives. "So the great dragon was cast out, that serpent of old, called the Devil and Satan, who deceives the whole world; he was cast to the earth, and his angels were cast out with him." (Revelation 12:9, NKJV)

It is only the truth that sets us free (John 8:32), and only obeying God's Word that keeps us safe from the enemy of our soul. These are eternal issues. Never forget, "the truth which abides in us… will be with us forever." (2John 1:2b)

## PRACTICAL GUIDELINES

1. *Never minimize the smallness of the misrepresentation.*
   Nineteen percent of those who took our *Church Wounds Survey* said they had been hurt by half-truths. However, the most startling aspect of their pain was not the enormity of the deception, but the smallness of the issue.

   It is greatly disturbing that a respected person would distort the truth about something infinitely small. Why would a leader risk his reputation over the seemingly minute? For this simple fact: if he would steal a penny, he would steal a dollar; if he would tell a so-called *white lie,* he would fabricate an entire story.

   In the end, truth always wins out, "For the proud will be humbled, but the humble will be honored." (Luke 14:11)

2.  *Ask others to hold you accountable.*
    Though this will be difficult, and highly embarrassing at times, ask
    a few courageous souls to point out when you seem to overstate or
    stretch the truth. Preciseness in truth-telling will make all of the
    difference in any relationship.

    "So humble yourselves under the mighty power of God, and in His
    good time He will honor you." (1 Peter 5:6)

3.  *Expose yourself.*
    Try and embarrass yourself regularly. It is a healthy exercise. We can
    all present our lives as pure as the driven snow. When we do this, we
    minimize our need for a Savior. We increase and our need for God
    decreases. I may have needed His help to get started in my Christ-
    likeness, but I'm on a roll now.

    How utterly deceptive!

    If we are really getting closer to the God who is light (1 John 1:5), then
    our imperfections should become more obvious instead of hidden.

    Don't be discouraged. No one knows our flaws better than God. He
    knew every sin we'd ever commit long before we were even born. And
    yet, His love for us never fluctuates. He never loves us more when we
    do right. Nor does He love us less when we do wrong. We are infinitely
    more than the sins we have committed or the mistakes we have made.

Before we write someone off, we should give them an opportunity to own
up to the words they have spoken. You will find, in many cases, men and
women of integrity will acknowledge when they have misspoken. For that
they should be commended. It takes courage to admit a mistake. You will
find that many are more committed to doing right than being right.

On the other hand, if a humble appeal has been made to acknowledge the truth and a Christian is unwilling to admit a deception, then we should follow the instructions in Scripture. Only after absolute certainty, should we follow Christ's admonition, "If your brother sins, go and show him his fault when the two of you are alone. If he listens to you, you have regained your brother. But if he does not listen, take one or two others with you, so that at the testimony of two or three witnesses every matter may be established. (Matthew 18:15–16, NET)

# INDISCRETION

*Section Four*

# FINANCIAL IMPROPRIETY

## CHAPTER ELEVEN: *David Loveless*

*"A former pastor wanted to alter a financial report to conceal his misuse of funds and manipulation of the finance committee. Another time deacons collected monthly dues from church auxiliaries on top of regular tithes and offerings with no accountability for the use of funds."*

*"After tithing and attending fifteen years, the church I grew up in denied my destitute mother and us kids from attending unless we paid $500 in 'absolution fees' because she and our father were divorcing. However, my dad, with assets of over a million dollars, was allowed to attend. The priest followed the money, not God."*

*"In my old church we raised $650,000 for a land purchase, then the money disappeared. Later the pastor bought a million dollar home after getting behind on his rent for another million dollar home owned by a church member."*

*"I attended one church for a number of years until the Sunday it decided to call out, without permission, people's names and the amounts they had given to the building program. Then the leaders shared the names of those who had not yet made a pledge. My family did not go back after that."*

*"A senior pastor I know forced a new sanctuary building project upon the congregation even though it was not supported or needed, all the while saying, 'God told me we are to do this.'"*

Like these who shared their stories in our *Church Wounds Survey*, if you have lived in the church world any length of time, you may have heard of or even personally experienced this type of situation. It is tragic that financial impropriety is ever spoken of in connection with Christ's Church.

Clearly we are commanded by God throughout the Bible to be givers: faithful, generous, Spirit-led, cheerful givers. Most of us seek to obey God in this. Most ministries and churches invest our offerings wisely, meeting the needs of others, while expanding the influence of the Kingdom of God here on Earth. When all goes according to God's plan, the Church stays out of the headlines. What makes the news and gets lodged in our minds is the dark side of the story.

Any time of the day or night we can flip on the television and find one or more ministries imploring us to "sow our financial seed" in the "good soil" of their project.

A problem arises when we invest our hard-earned resources into "good soil" only later to discover that the soil was "soiled." Our generation has had a vault load of dirty money disasters.

## FALL OF THE CROOKED EMPIRES

Maybe you recall a 1980s televangelist who was convicted of 24 counts of fraud and conspiracy and given a forty-five year prison sentence. The nationally known leader was accused of defrauding the mostly working class ministry partners of his television network out of $158 million.

Just how the televangelist stole from those he led in Christ's name captivated the nation's attention and epitomized a decade of similar scandals. While the hunger for the latest televangelist exposé has receded some from the national spotlight (at least for the moment), incidents of financial impropriety continue to plague the Christian Church landscape.

According to Matt Kennedy in a *Newsday* article for the Associated Baptist Press, 20 percent of American congregations and ministries lose money to unscrupulous church leaders.

- Two executives from a Baptist Foundation in Arizona were indicted on fraud and racketeering after more than 11,000 investors lost more than $550 million. It is perhaps the largest case of Christian fraud in American history. The men were accused of publishing favorable financial statements to retain investments while they shifted bad assets to "off-the-books" companies in order to hide the foundation's extensive losses from auditors.

- In Kentucky, a pastor pleaded guilty to stealing $730,000 from his congregation. The *Cincinnati Enquirer* reported that, as part of the plea agreement, prosecutors dropped three counts of income-tax evasion and two counts of transferring stolen church money across state lines.

- In Washington, D.C., a watchdog group called *Citizens for Responsibility and Ethics* recently filed two complaints with the IRS against a pastor in Minneapolis. The second complaint was based on documents obtained by the *Minnesota Monitor* claiming the pastor bought a plane from the church and then leased it back to the church for almost $900,000 a year.

Has every minister turned crook? Of course not! Can any designated financiers of the church be trusted? Certainly! The statistics show the vast majority of churches are upright in their financial approach, exchanging ordinary dollars into rich, life-giving ministry.

In my own church, elders, finance teams, staff members, and I have witnessed countless budget meetings over the years where we submitted to the rigorous, tedious and, truthfully, expensive process of making sure every dollar is accounted for and used for its maximum impact. Ministries worldwide, on a regular basis, share this same process. But mistakes can happen.

## WHAT WE DON'T KNOW CAN HURT US

Dalen Jackson, associate professor of Biblical Studies at the Baptist Seminary of Kentucky, says many instances of financial misappropriation are truly unintentional. He says they happen due to laziness, tax law misunderstandings, or just carelessness. Think about it: if this sometimes occurs to you and me and to thousands everyday in the business world, we should also expect it will happen to well-meaning churches and ministries.

Steve Clifford is a financial planner who specializes in clergy tax returns. He said that of the more than 10,000 tax returns he has filed involving clergy, only one misappropriation of funds has surfaced. In that case, Clifford said, it was clear the minister was guilty of sloppiness, not wrong doing.

"Greed is a temptation for anyone but not for most of the pastors I work with," Clifford said. "Most of them are self-sacrificing."

### WHO'S ROBBING GOD?

Financial impropriety is not only committed by those in the Church receiving tithes and offerings, but also by those giving. Remember, Ananias and Sapphira came to tragic ends when they were discovered withholding money from their spiritual community after the sale of some property and lying about it to the Apostle Peter. (Acts 5:1–11)

Let us remember, as we piously challenge the financial propriety of others in the Christian community, to keep our eyes on our own bankbooks. Are *we* as faithful to share with those truly in need? Do *we* hold back tithes and offerings using God's portion of our income for other, lesser purposes? Have *we* personally misappropriated any of the resources God has earmarked for His Kingdom?

### HEALING THE WOUND OF FINANCIAL MISCONDUCT

Whether you were wounded in the church by intentional or unintentional financial mishandlings, here are some steps to consider for emotional and spiritual repair.

First, forgive and release those who have mismanaged any amount of ministry funds for any reason. The fact remains—people are going to mess up with our money, *just like we do*. The Bible commands us, *no matter the issue,* we are to forgive, "seventy times seven." (Matthew 18:22) However, if you have forgiven and humbly approached the offenders in the Biblical fashion of Matthew 8 and the misconduct continues, prayerfully consider finding a new church as God would lead you.

Next, find a church you can trust and invest joyously with them. Most ministries are far above reproach in this area and exhaust themselves to make sure they are faithful stewards of every dime entrusted to them. Still, there's always a margin of trust when you write someone a check. Which leads me to my final step.

Once you've given any amount of money *to the Lord*, release it totally to His discretion. In fact, technically, you have not given your money to a church but returned some portion of it to your Master to whom it ultimately belongs. My job as a citizen of the kingdom is to obey the Lord as a faithful, generous giver. It is also my job to invest as wisely as I can by observing the results over a long period of time. This is why my wife and I love giving tithes and offerings in our local church. We can watch our money make an eternal difference in people's lives.

Give to churches and ministries that are annually audited. You can either call or email ministries to ask if an independent board audits them. If necessary, request a copy of their annual report.

## CHECKS AND BALANCES

In financial accounting, an audit is an independent assessment of the fairness by which a company's management presents its financial statements. Competent, independent, and objective people, known as auditors or accountants, issue a report based on the results of the audit. The auditor's report reflects accepted standards set by governing bodies that regulate ministries.

Because of the complexity and expertise required to obtain these audits, large churches are required to pay thousands of dollars each year to keep a clean bill of health. It is a cost most are willing to pay to alleviate fear and doubt from contributors. You should be aware that some ministries may be financially upright but do not submit themselves to audits because of the large cost involved. For these situations find out if the ministry employs any other type of annual, financial review.

As God's Word commands, give cheerfully, generously, and sacrificially but don't become consumed in a financial witch-hunt. There is no joy in giving if our hearts are clouded with suspicion of greed or impropriety. Once you have returned your offerings to the Lord release them to the caretaking of trusted, godly leaders who will steward them well. If you often feel uneasy or distrusting, move your giving to a local church you can joyfully support.

"For from time to time those who owned lands or houses sold them, brought the money from the sales and put it at the apostles' feet, and it was distributed to anyone as he had need." (Acts 4:34–35, NIV)

### Q & A

*Q: How do churches decide on staff salaries?*

A: The Bible provides several guidelines, including the following passage:

"The elders who direct the affairs of the church well are worthy of double honor, especially those whose work is preaching and teaching. For the Scripture says, 'Do not muzzle the ox while it is treading out the grain,' and 'The worker deserves his wages.'" (1 Timothy 5:17–18, NIV)

In some churches, the pastors themselves decide. In others, the decision is made by the denomination. But in most financially accountable ministries, an independent board of financially and spiritually minded people determines staff salaries based upon a series of factors including:

- An analysis of national norms, guidelines for staff salaries, and benefits provided through independent agencies such as the yearly updated book, *The National Compensation Guide for Church Staffs*. These are based on a compiled national survey of churches of all sizes and denominations including location and total budget, load of responsibilities, length of time served, quality and quantity of contribution, formal and non-formal education, and other factors.

- The significance of the position to the overall health and growth of the church.

- The size of the church's budget.

When I was growing up in a small town parsonage, my father's pastor lifestyle reflected the conviction of the Church at the time. Most churches literally expected their pastors to save the world on a dime a day. Congregations rarely considered the financial needs of a pastor's family. In many instances, an oppressive financial environment was intended to keep the pastor poor and humble, free from the "love of money." Usually such a situation backfired as providing for his family became as high a priority as spiritually providing for the church.

On the flip side, the Bible makes it clear that church leaders disqualify themselves if they demonstrate an obsession for money. But who wants the job of examining a pastor? That is a very slippery slope. (*See Chapter 18 on Judgmentalism.*)

*Q: Jesus didn't carry cash, did He? When He sent His disciples out, He did so without issuing money. So why should we pay pastors and church staff?*

A: Let's look at the cultural climate in Jesus' day. In 1st century Middle Eastern culture, the standard practice was to provide shelter, food, and basic needs for traveling rabbis. Communities regularly supported religious leaders seeking to serve them and Jehovah.

*Q: The Apostle Paul was a tentmaker and said he didn't want to be a financial burden to the church. Shouldn't all pastors be 'tentmakers'?*

A: Paul, who, as far as we know, was single during his church ministry and had no family to fund, voluntarily chose not to take money from the churches he served. In part, this was to prove his single-minded motive to share the gospel. What money he did collect subsidized the expansion of the kingdom in other places. So it is not surprising that Paul penned directive words to Timothy (1 Timothy 5:17–18) and the leaders of the church at Ephesus, with similar instructions to Titus (1:7) that elders are not to "pursue dishonest gain."

A church can make decisions about its pastor(s) being a "tentmaker" based upon the time demands of the position and the funds available. "But be sure that everything is done properly and in order." (1 Corinthians 14:40) Giving "respect and honor to all to whom it is due." (Romans 13:7)

# IMMORALITY

## CHAPTER TWELVE: *Francis Anfuso*

*"The essence of immorality is the tendency to make an exception of myself."*
—Jane Addams, First American Woman Nobel Peace Prize Laureate

My father was an unfaithful man.

From the beginning of his 37-year marriage to my mother, his infidelities were a destructive pattern in the fabric of their relationship. When my mom sought support from her own father, who himself struggled with sexual improprieties, his advice was, "Does he beat you? Does he give you money? Then stay with him." Sadly, this type of twisted counsel perpetuates generational bondage.

My father was a successful politician, congressman, and state Supreme Court justice. His middle name L'Episcopo means, "the bishop." Still he was unable to control his passions or lead our family. It is highly likely that on the night he died of a massive heart attack in a New York City hotel room, he was being unfaithful.

As an atheist from ages 15 to 22, my own moral failings led to an STD, two abortions, and a trail of destruction that still embarrass me decades later. Coming to Jesus with hopes of living a sexually pure life seemed incredible. From the moment I surrendered my will to God I have had to guard my heart with all diligence, for it affects every aspect of my fragile life. (Proverbs 4:23)

Early in my Christian life I watched my best friend in the Lord fall into sexual sin. It broke my heart and made me wonder if I would fair any better.

Even my first speaking engagement as a traveling minister provided a glimpse into the enemy's strategy to destroy me. As I stood on the platform to worship, the organist blatantly flirted with me. When I told the pastor, he struggled to believe it since she was his daughter-in-law. Within a couple of years, however, she would seduce another minister. Divorce followed.

In spite of the devil's attempts to destroy my life in Christ, by the protecting grace and power of a faithful God, I have never been romantically inappropriate with anyone. For 34 years I have cherished a relationship with my beautiful wife, Suzie. Our two lovely daughters and sons-in-law love the Lord and are training four gorgeous grandchildren who will inherit many extraordinary blessings.

Though I am certainly a sinner who daily fights the battle for purity of mind, I have been saved by the grace and mercy of a holy God. He keeps me morally faithful. For "I know the One in whom I trust, and I am sure that He is able to guard what I have entrusted to Him until the day of His return." (2Timothy 1:12b)

While I have breath, I will trust Jesus to keep me.

## TREACHEROUS TRAVELS

My wife, children and I had the privilege of traveling around the world, preaching the good news of Jesus Christ for nearly two decades. During that season we met many godly and morally faithful leaders in the Body of Christ. They modeled healthy relationships in a world sorely lacking this priceless quality.

Unfortunately, on more than one occasion, we were grieved to encounter moral failures amongst leaders that ravaged marriages, families, churches and even whole communities. Time and again, someone highly esteemed, a pillar amongst equals, had fallen. As the classic poem states, "But there is no joy in Mudville—mighty Casey has struck out."[9]

---

9    Thayer EL. Casey at the Bat. San Francisco Examiner. June 3, 1888.

Though many fall in obscurity, prominent personalities who succumb to moral failure torment our hopes most. Politicians, entertainers, athletes, and celebrities from every background can fall into moral disrepute, bringing horrendous reproach upon their families and supporters. But when a minister of the Lord Jesus Christ, someone claiming righteousness, falls from grace, we are crushed with bitter disappointment to discover a double-life, a breech of trust.

The unthinkable has happened!

The leader we respected, who modeled attributes of God's character has fallen prey to immorality, a violation still regarded as the depth of betrayal.

I don't think I have encountered a greater degree of disillusionment than when I look into the eyes of a defrauded spouse, an abandoned child, or a congregation awakened to the horrible truth.

In our *Church Wounds Survey*, 18 percent of respondents said that immorality within the church inflicted one of the greatest hurts they suffered.

What can be more painful than being wounded by a father or a friend?

### SETTING THE BAR HIGH

It would be impossible to hide the fact that leaders in the Bible gave in to sexual immorality. Samson, David, and Solomon stood as pillars of hope, only to fall victim to their lusts.

Even in our day, many notable followers of Jesus once made marvelous headlines in God's name. Now yellowed newspapers remember the shame they brought to millions of faithful followers of Jesus.

It takes months, even years, to build something that can stand for decades. And yet a few thoughtless, selfish moments, can tear it down in an instant.

But not just our spiritual leaders are tainted.

An x-ray of the moral backbone of many would-be Christians today reveals chronic double-mindedness that causes repulsion rather than interest to a skeptical world. A recent survey of such Christians is nothing short of alarming.

> *When asked to identify their activities over the last thirty days, born-again believers were just as likely to bet or gamble, to visit a pornographic website, to take something that did not belong to them, to consult a medium or psychic, to physically fight or abuse someone, to have consumed enough alcohol to be considered legally drunk, to have used an illegal, nonprescription drug, to have said something to someone that was not true, to have gotten back at someone for something he or she did, and to have said mean things behind another person's back. No difference.*

> *One study we conducted examined Americans' engagement in some type of sexually inappropriate behavior, including looking at online pornography, viewing sexually explicit magazines or movies, or having an intimate sexual encounter outside of marriage. In all, we found that 30 percent of born-again Christians admitted to at least one of these activities in the past thirty days, compared with 35 percent of other Americans.[10]*

No wonder people mock Christians openly. No wonder they tell us to live it or be quiet.

It is also why Jesus told us to first remove the Giant Sequoia from our own eye, before we will have the credibility to help remove the tiny splinter from the lives of others. (Matthew 7:5) The Bible admonishes, "Let there be no sexual immorality, impurity, or greed among you. Such sins have no place among God's people." (Ephesians 5:3)

This is actually how plagues of immorality are conceived. "And we must not engage in sexual immorality as some of them did, causing 23,000 of them to die in one day." (1Corinthians 10:8)

As the patriarch, Joseph, ran for his life when Potiphar's wife tried to seduce him (Genesis 39), so should we. "Flee sexual immorality. Every sin that a man does is outside the body, but he who commits sexual immorality sins

---

10    Kinnaman D, Lyons G. unChristian: What a New Generation Really Thinks about Christianity… and Why It Matters. Grand Rapids, MI: Baker Publishing Group; 2007.

against his own body. Or do you not know that your body is the temple of the Holy Spirit who is in you, whom you have from God, and you are not your own? For you were bought at a price; therefore glorify God in your body and in your spirit, which are God's." (1Corinthians 6:18–20, NKJV)

Our moral purity must not reside in word and deed alone, but in thought as well. Jesus said, "You have heard the commandment that says, 'You must not commit adultery.' But I say, anyone who even looks at a woman with lust has already committed adultery with her in his heart. So if your eye—even your good eye—causes you to lust, gouge it out and throw it away. It is better for you to lose one part of your body than for your whole body to be thrown into hell. And if your hand—even your stronger hand—causes you to sin, cut it off and throw it away. It is better for you to lose one part of your body than for your whole body to be thrown into hell." (Matthew 5:27–30)

This standard of inner purity can plague us who have histories of mental contamination. Yet, the unapologetic words of Jesus challenge all hearers to live no longer as hypocrites. Speaking of the religious leaders of His day, Jesus stated, "Every plant not planted by my heavenly Father will be uprooted, so ignore them. They are blind guides leading the blind, and if one blind person guides another, they will both fall into a ditch." (Matthew 15:13–14) "For from the heart come evil thoughts, murder, adultery, all sexual immorality, theft, lying, and slander. These are what defile you." (Matthew 15:19–20a)

We must not let the high bar discourage us, but rather inspire us to yield to the Holy Spirit, Who alone can keep us.

**SEXUAL SINS OF PRIESTS**

The random immorality of priests goes back thousands of years.

Those who have been favored by both God and man have found they are prime targets of a relentless enemy. These passionate souls must vigilantly resist the seductions of their lower nature. "Now the works of the flesh are obvious: sexual immorality, impurity, depravity." (Galatians 5:19, NET)

The words of Jesus increase the sense of urgency, especially in our own day, "if the light you think you have is actually darkness, how deep that darkness is!" (Matthew 6:23b) May the light we have come from God alone!

In the beginning of the Old Testament, Eli was a high priest in Israel. Given the spiritual authority to lead God's people into right relationship with their Creator, Eli was unable to lead even his own sons who likewise served as priests in God's house. "Now Eli was very old, but he was aware of what his sons were doing to the people of Israel. He knew, for instance, that his sons were seducing the young women who assisted at the entrance of the Tabernacle. Eli said to them, 'I have been hearing reports from all the people about the wicked things you are doing. Why do you keep sinning? You must stop, my sons! The reports I hear among the Lord's people are not good. If someone sins against another person, God can mediate for the guilty party. But if someone sins against the Lord, who can intercede?' But Eli's sons wouldn't listen to their father, for the Lord was already planning to put them to death." (1Samuel 2:22–25)

The Lord then spoke to the young prophet Samuel about the impending judgment upon Eli and his rebellious sons. "I have warned him [Eli] that judgment is coming upon his family forever, because his sons are blaspheming God and he hasn't disciplined them. So I have vowed that the sins of Eli and his sons will never be forgiven by sacrifices or offerings." (1Samuel 3:13–14) "Therefore, the Lord, the God of Israel, says: I promised that your branch of the tribe of Levi would always be my priests. But I will honor those who honor me, and I will despise those who think lightly of me. The time is coming when I will put an end to your family, so it will no longer serve as my priests. All the members of your family will die before their time. None will reach old age." (1Samuel 3:30–31)

Chilling!

What is the root cause of this perilous seduction, this hidden cancer that unravels even the most promising life? Jesus asserted, "God's light came into the world, but people loved the darkness more than the light, for their actions were evil. All who do evil hate the light and refuse to go near it for fear their sins will be exposed. But those who do what is right come to the light so others can see that they are doing what God wants." (John 3:19b–21)

We have all experienced the consequence of doing wrong. But not all sins induce comparable repercussions. "We who teach will be judged by God with greater strictness." (James 3:1b)

When a spiritual leader looks to God to fulfill a need for intimacy, and yet in one supremely foolish moment casts off restraint that would have preserved his destiny, all respect and trust evaporates. By flinging away moral integrity for a few minutes of shallow pleasure, he forfeits a worthy reputation and a priceless future. The scope of this tragedy can never be minimized. Keep the guaranteed catastrophic backlash ever in front, and escape sabotaging your entire life. Even more importantly, by filling our hearts and minds with the living Spirit and Word of God will we be able to "submit to God… resist the devil and he will flee." (James 4:7b, NET)

If you have been wounded by the moral failure of others, don't allow their stumbling to trip you up. Don't let their deception deceive you.

Ask God for His heart. God "was merciful and forgave their sins and did not destroy them all. Many times He held back His anger and did not unleash His fury! For He remembered that they were merely mortal, gone like a breath of wind that never returns." (Psalm 78:38–39)

# INAPPROPRIATE
# BEHAVIOR

## CHAPTER THIRTEEN: *Francis Anfuso*

*"Moses…commanded us that such should be stoned. But, what do You say?"*
*Jesus replied, "He who is without sin among you, let him throw a stone at her first."*
(John 8:5, 7, NKJV)

I cannot begin to write this chapter without first thinking of my own inappropriate behavior. At times I hurt others without cause and said things that wounded, especially those closest to me. I don't need to think of anyone guiltier than myself.

Yet, before your imagination wonders what diabolical atrocities I have committed, let me add that they were so serious they brought excruciating pain to the one who loved me most. Pain on every level: physical, emotional, relational—all caused by me and my inappropriate behavior. I am grieved to think that my sin, in some unconscionable way, stumbled many others. That somewhere in the residue of past choices I have left a stain of hurt and misrepresentation that caused people to move away from God, not toward Him.

I have needed a lot of help processing my past, both inappropriate behavior that I imposed and that I endured. But I was marvelously rescued from the indiscretions I could not undo. Someone is able to comfort those I have discomforted, even to gladden those I have saddened.

I needed a Savior.

My prayer is that all those I have hurt will realize this as well.

You would think that after making such forthright admissions, my life would be filled with regret, but it is not. It is filled with rejoicing; for God is able to transcend time and space to aid those I have lost track of. My greatest mistakes have all been washed away and no longer bring pain to the God I offended most. This brings me to perhaps the most comforting of all the *Church Wounds Survey* statistics. Though 86 percent of respondents admitted they had been wounded, a miraculous 70 percent acknowledged they were mostly healed.

How gracious is our God! "For we do not have a great High Priest who cannot sympathize with our weaknesses, but was in all points tempted as we are, yet without sin." (Hebrews 4:15, NKJV)

He understands!

As you read the comments of those who have been slighted, bruised, and even abused, think of yourself—think of Jesus—and believe that His grace is able to cover all.

Never forget: love covers!

## A MOUNTAIN OF MISDEEDS

The facts are in. Surveys amongst those in and outside of the church definitively prove there's a whole lot of inappropriate behavior going on—and it hasn't gone unnoticed by those on either side. David Kinnaman's and Gabe Lyons' 2007 book, *unChristian: What a New Generation Really Thinks About Christianity . . . and Why It Matters,* states so clearly, "Even though our words at times do not match our actions, we must not dumb down the jolting challenge our words inflict upon our waffling will."[11]

"Among young outsiders, 84 percent say they personally know at least one committed Christian. Yet just 15 percent thought the lifestyles of those Christ followers were significantly different from the norm. This gap speaks volumes."[12]

---

11    Kinnaman D, Lyons G. unChristian: What a New Generation Really Thinks about Christianity…
      and Why It Matters. Grand Rapids, MI: Baker Publishing Group; 2007.

12    Kinnaman D, Lyons G. unChristian: What a New Generation Really Thinks about Christianity…
      and Why It Matters. Grand Rapids, MI: Baker Publishing Group; 2007.

Our own *Church Wounds Survey* found nothing different:

> *"Several of the people that attended my last church would go to Bible studies and Sunday services, and then be seen misrepresenting Christ: drinking, drugs, adultery, etc."*

> *"I was very involved as a teenager in my church. My pastor groped me from behind at a picnic one summer. I never did anything or said anything about it because it was one of those things where you just say to yourself, 'Did that just happen?' He acted as if nothing happened so I did too. It took many years of being angry with God and then going to Christian counseling for me to recover from these wounds. I have learned to trust God again."*

> *"I helped start a church with a narcissist who misused his prophetic gifting to manipulate the men and women in the church to be dependent on him, instead of Christ, for their healing. He also lied to many of the women in the church and manipulated them into submitting to him sexually 'as part of their healing.'"*

> *"My favorite pastor when I was growing up left the church abruptly because he had been caught cheating on his wife."*

Person after person related a familiar pattern. Though wounds are everywhere, time doesn't heal—only Jesus does.


### UNPACKING PAIN

A thirty-something female described the root of her defilement in our survey, "I have been violated by a leader emotionally and physically. This was devastating!" She frankly described what devastated her most: "When leaders, who needed integrity preyed on the young innocent who trusted them."

What can be crueler than a *predator* pretending to be a *protector?*

Other inappropriate behaviors may not seem quite as reprehensible, but can still have significant repercussions. An older Christian wrote about a childhood wounding. "When I was a teen in Sunday School, I had learning disabilities at a time when learning disabilities were not recognized. I faithfully studied my Sunday School lesson every Saturday night. On Sunday, the teacher asked questions but I answered them wrong. At the end of the class, he looked at me and said in front of the whole class, 'Next time study your lesson!' I was so embarrassed, I wanted to leave church."

Though it is not likely that we will maintain appropriate conduct at all times, sensitivity to the Holy Spirit will alert us to acknowledge and seek reconciliation from those we have hurt.

On the other hand, in order to receive complete healing from yesterday's wounds, we must be vigilant to ask God to touch the deepest recesses of our pain. He longs to do this more than we know. The formerly wounded teenager quoted above added, "At a later age, in my thirties, I was introduced to a ministry that taught me to hear from God, share my feelings with God, and receive his care for me. I have completely forgiven this individual and can tell the story without any emotional reaction. At the time, I did not think God liked me very much because my parents didn't affirm me. I have learned God loves me and really cares about what happens to me. It took me nearly a year and a half to believe that God loved me."

A scripture she said helped in her healing process was Psalm 71:20–21, "Though You have made me see troubles, many and bitter, You will restore my life again; from the depths of the earth You will again bring me up. You will increase my honor and comfort me once again." The pain she had been through gave her a passion, which in turn led to God's greater purpose and plan for her life. Along the way, she encountered further dimensions in her healing process, "We joined a home group where people really loved and cared for others. They reached out to affirm each other."

Though it is painful to listen to horrific stories, it is at times essential to exercise patience so that battered souls may be heard. One struggling survey participant wrote, "Sometimes I try to express what has happened to me to leaders in the church, some horrible things. I sense, as I start to speak, a disinterest, or leaders trying to hurry up their conversation so they can get on their way. So, I stop sharing!"

I have to admit, I have done this.

I have misjudged the need of the moment. I have fast-forwarded someone who, with a little more patience, could have sufficiently expressed his or her heart to a pastor they hoped would have time for them. If I had only been more sensitive, I could have helped replace the fixed impression of a leader who didn't care enough to listen.

Just a little more time—a little more kindness—a little more Christ-likeness.

Other opportunities will certainly be ahead.

## LACKLUSTER LEADERS

Many of the hundreds of church wounds were very similar. "My pastor was found to be viewing pornography online. It seemed like he could be too friendly with young women in our church. When confronted with these problems he denied them, shifted blame, and fired staff. As a result the church was taken over by the assistant pastor. He turned out to be just as bad in different ways. He was arrogant, proud, condescending, manipulative, and mean."

What was the fallout of the inappropriate behavior of these two leaders?

The writer continued, "My spiritual innocence was taken away. When I saw the first pastor again a year or so later, he could only talk about how the assistant pastor had hurt him and how he was wronged. He had no idea, nor was he concerned about how he, by his actions, had destroyed a whole community of people. I was still hurting from the whole thing, as I know others were, while he simply moved on to the next stage of life. Also, this man has since started another church. It's hard to understand how God could allow him to be active again in ministry when he never publicly repented for his actions. (I was part of a committee to search for the new pastor so I know more than most.) I know friends who go to his church whom he has taken money from and would not repay. It seems like he continues in the same pattern. Why would God allow that?"

Only God knows the reasons why He exercises restraint, and grants seemingly excessive time for people to repent. His Word provides a glimpse into His thoughts and intentions, and thus His very nature. Many of us have awakened late to a personal deception and the agonizing journey of unraveling sin. More often than not, we have a clear read on the sins of others long before we fully embrace our own. Yet, God knew all of our sins, even before one of them was committed.

Did He hold this against us?

Did He think less of us because of our shortcomings?

With infinite foreknowledge, God allows lackluster leaders to lead lackluster people. For what purpose, you ask? So that, in the end, the whole hodge-podge of hurt can work for the good of everyone involved. Though this miraculous healing sequence can only happen if a person is willing to see from God's perspective, the miracle is: *it can and does happen.*

God, our Redeemer, can redeem everything!

God, our Healer, can heal anyone!

Pointless pain can vanquish, but purposeful pain can bear extraordinary fruit. The challenge is: we alone get to choose if our pain will be purposeful or pointless.

### OUR LONG-SUFFERING LOVER

God's patience and long-suffering are infinitely beyond our comprehension, but should never wander beyond our appreciation. We chaff when God appears to move too slowly in correcting or even judging others. Yet, are we filled with gratitude when we are spared well-deserved retribution?

Speaking about the grace of God, Paul, the former persecutor of Christians wrote to non-Jews (Gentiles), "Therefore consider the goodness and severity of God: on those who fell, severity; but toward you, goodness, if you continue in His goodness. Otherwise you also will be cut off." (Romans 11:22, NKJV)

God judges sin severely. Consider the crucifixion of Jesus. Our sinless Creator suffered and died in our place for sins we committed. What irony that we, the perpetrators of sin, will never be the recipients of their judgment. We are, instead, the beneficiaries of a reward God alone deserves. This goodness is endless if we allow God's sinless nature to cover our sin.

The Bible is not squeamish in addressing the inappropriate behavior of fallen man. Rather it meticulously tracks the flawless behavior of a gracious God, and His unending efforts to see His broken sons and daughters fully restored. It is the seemingly impossible story of the greatest rescue mission of all time: how countless individuals suddenly awakened to the reality that their sins, though many, had been forgiven.

If we maintain a *victim posture,* then we will never know the boundless liberty of becoming a pardoned *villain.* We are a nation of villains, claiming to be victims. Resurrection life is reserved for those willing to admit their crimes against a holy God.

The Old Testament prophet Ezra confessed, "For we were slaves. Yet our God did not forsake us in our bondage; but He extended mercy to us." (Ezra 9:9a, NKJV)

The psalmist shares his own deep appreciation for God's merciful kindness, "For You, Lord, are good, and ready to forgive, and abundant in mercy to all those who call upon You." (Psalm 86:5, NKJV)

I am far more villain than victim. Thus, being fully pardoned makes me far more grateful than sad.

How about you?

What have you chosen to believe? Do you believe that you are the unfairly treated victim of wounded Earth, or the undeserving recipient of the perfect love offered to all by the heavenly Cross of Calvary?

The former misconception makes you miss the entire reason Jesus came.

The latter reality makes the God of the Universe the only true victim.

# LEADER INSENSITIVITY

## CHAPTER FOURTEEN: *David Loveless*

In a church staff meeting I listened as one of our teams outlined a passionate proposal for significant change in its ministry. Throughout the otherwise excellent presentation I found myself distracted by a condescending tone underpinning the discussion. I knew the team had labored and prayed over this meeting. It was paramount for the next phase of their work. I just did not understand the edginess.

When they finished, I told the group I appreciated their hard work and agreed on the content of their proposal. I then decided to challenge them on several critical points. This should not have surprised them. Advising leaders is part of my job. Then I ended with what seemed to me as a minor lecture on the poor choice of tone in their talk. The team left the room with little out of the ordinary. However, that night I found out they were devastated.

It rarely sits well with me when people who need coaching baulk at pure instruction. But what I really dislike is facing the truth that, as a leader, I have been overbearing or unkind with my instruction.

Here is what some who took our survey reported:

> *"In an email, a youth leader responded with mean comments when I asked if it was okay to attend a Bible study not affiliated with our church. When I confronted him about his harsh words, he told me he sends a lot of emails and didn't remember his comments."*

> *"Some years ago my ex-husband was abusive to the point of attempting to strangle me. When I told this to one of our pastors he said, 'It only happened twice.' Then he gave me a book called How to Save Your Marriage By Yourself."*

*"Leaders in a church I once attended were too forceful about directing people to serve. I had only been attending one month when I was told, not asked, to do the introduction and benediction of a service. Even after I expressed reluctance to participate based on discomfort and inadequate knowledge the leader remained determined I should."*

*"Our pastor used our marital problems as an example without asking our permission."*

It may not surprise you that of the 26 categories we target in our *Church Wounds Survey,* "leader insensitivities" landed as the second most common church wound with 40 percent of the respondents acknowledging this.

### CAUSES OF LEADER INSENSITIVITY

It was during a mid-afternoon staff meeting, one of my first as a youth leader in a large church, when the senior pastor became enraged. Certain staff had failed to do follow up calls with all the church visitors from the previous week. After citing large workloads and special projects the pastor had assigned as reasons for the delay, the pastor replied, "Don't make excuses!"

In the comedy, *The Devil Wears Prada,* a naïve young woman scores a job as the assistant to one of the nations biggest, albeit ruthless and tyrannical, fashion magazine editors. Everyone in the theater found the movie hilarious. I think this was for two reasons: 1) we all knew leaders like that and 2) at that particular moment the editor was inflicting madness on someone else.

The entitlement the editor carried reminded me of many church bosses I have known. As they walk down a hall, waters part and their minions scurry. These forceful preachers and leaders sport stern intensity for the vital role they play in the Kingdom. They seem faintly aware of anyone else. Those they employ often resign in search of calmer conditions.

The Bible knows these leaders well. Saul. Herod. Nebuchadnezzar. Pharaoh. Potiphar—and, not to exclude the ladies, Sarah.

*Now Sarai, Abram's wife, had borne him no children. But she had an Egyptian maidservant named Hagar; so she said to Abram, "The LORD has kept me from having children. Go, sleep with my maidservant; perhaps I can build a family through her." Abram agreed to what Sarai said. So after Abram had been living in Canaan ten years, Sarai his wife took her Egyptian maidservant Hagar and gave her to her husband to be his wife. He slept with Hagar, and she conceived. When she knew she was pregnant, she began to despise her mistress. Then Sarai said to Abram, "You are responsible for the wrong I am suffering. I put my servant in your arms, and now that she knows she is pregnant, she despises me. May the LORD judge between you and me." "Your servant is in your hands," Abram said. "Do with her whatever you think best." Then Sarai mistreated Hagar; so she fled from her. The angel of the LORD found Hagar near a spring in the desert; it was the spring that is beside the road to Shur. And he said, "Hagar, servant of Sarai, where have you come from, and where are you going?" "I'm running away from my mistress Sarai," she answered. (Genesis 16:1–8, NIV)*

Sarai, later renamed Sarah, was the leading female influencer in her tribe. She was a driven woman with a clear agenda. Laser-focused on her God-promised son she was hurt by her inability to conceive. Being the take-charge woman she was, when things didn't go her way, she devised an alternate route.

Most church leaders I know are not scheming, power-driven brutes. They are passionate, Christ-centered shepherds who sometimes say the wrong thing.

### OOPS, THERE IT IS

One weekend while speaking, I referenced Truet Cathey, the founder of Chick-fil-A. I have always said, despite its high calorie content, Chick-fil-A is this pastor's food of choice. But there I was in passionate discourse about the origins of Chick-fil-A and I mentioned that its first location in Atlanta was called The Dwarf House. Don't ask me why I felt this tidbit of information was so important. But as this comment left my mouth, I spied on the fourth row a very small adult person whose day job happened to be playing one of the seven dwarf characters at Walt Disney World.

Who would be that insensitive? I would never make light of people with any physical difference or disability. But to all who noticed, my relational IQ that day looked about 90 points below 100. After the service, I introduced myself to this first-time guest and apologized for my horrible but unintentional insensitivity.

The man never came back.

### A GIFT THAT KEEPS ON GIVING

Sometimes we perceive leaders to be uncaring when their behavior may be fanned by their spiritual gift or temperament. A simple understanding of personality types and spiritual gift motivations goes a long way in every relationship, and with leaders it's no different. At our most basic emotional level we are all introverts, extroverts, or a combination of both.

Many excellent *introverted leaders* are misjudged for appearing withdrawn. Actually, introverts lose emotional energy the longer they are with others. The larger the group, the faster the leakage! At some point, they withdraw as a means of self-preservation. This sometimes comes across as rejecting or not caring for others. Truthfully, the leader just needs to get alone to regroup so he or she can return again refreshed.

An *extroverted leader* can be an excessive talker, crowding people's space, appearing overbearing, or lacking boundaries. Being with lots of people feeds extroverts as much as it depletes introverts. Because it's easy for them, extroverts sometimes push others into upfront positions or leadership activities. In all their excitement sometimes they over-promise and under-deliver.

When it comes to spiritual motivations, the Bible says some of us are gifted to lead, teach, administrate, or offer hospitality. And some are gifted with mercy. Guess which leaders will be most sensitive to people? Those beautiful, caring, mercy-energized folks; God bless them! May their tribe increase!

An interesting dichotomy in the Kingdom of God is that while we may not have the gift of giving, we are all called to give. We may not have the gift of hospitality, but we are to be hospitable. And we may not have the gift of mercy, but we are commanded to be merciful. Whether or not it's our primary spiritual motivator, we are all exhorted to express any aspect of the character of Christ God asks of us, confident that what He requires He will also empower.

## HAVE YOU SEEN THESE LEADERS?

There are many ways in which leaders can wound the Church. Our *Church Wounds Survey* respondents described a variety of hurtful situations. Perhaps you can relate to an experience in which a leader may have:

- Expected his or her volunteers to do much more than he or she originally communicated.

- Started meetings and events later than scheduled and did not apologize to those that sacrificed to be on time.

- Ended meetings and events later than communicated, assuming these meetings should have taken priority for those who attended.

- Was so task-driven on a project that he or she seemed to care more about the project itself than the needs of the people who were helping with the project.

- Failed to comprehend how much time, money, or people it would take to get a job done.

- Blasted past people he or she knows—being too rushed and distracted to acknowledge them.

- Failed to call about or even ask about a crisis a small group member was experiencing.

- Made an insensitive joke at an attendee's expense.

- Piled on guilt over people already feeling bad for not measuring up.

### BINDING THE WOUNDS OF INSENSITIVITY

You might have read the above list and discovered you shared a wounding in common with others hurt by leader insensitivity. Diagnosing your pain is the first step. The next steps follow.

*1. Know God sees you and cares deeply. He will make a way to get it right.*

Although the story of Sarai and Hagar is sad, a significant truth is that the Lord saw the wrong done by the leader and deeply cared about the one mistreated. He came to comfort and encourage Hagar and tell her He would make up for whatever she lacked through her circumstance.

"The angel added, 'I will increase your descendants that they will be too numerous to count.' She gave this name to the Lord who spoke to her, 'You are the God who sees me,' for she said, 'I have now seen the One who sees me.'" (Genesis 16:10,13, NIV)

*2. When a leader is insensitive, let them know in love.*

Blind spots for a driver can cause serious accidents. Some leaders are completely in the dark about the way they come across, ending in the same devastating result. They need us to turn a light on for them. Meet with the person and tell him you believe he wants to be a caring, sensitive leader. But you want him to know that his care is not consistently communicated by how he treats people around him. Don't be vague. Go prepared to give the leader several specific examples. Focus on your feelings. Avoid saying, "you shouldn't have," or " you always." Instead say, "When you did_____, it made me feel_____."

Most leaders have no desire to be insensitive. We all need people who will love us enough to help us learn how we have hurt them. I want to grow more like Jesus as a leader. But as much as I desire that, I cannot do it alone.

*3. Check your own sensitivity.*

Sometimes, the very thing that bugs us most about others is the issue we struggle with as well. Folks get upset with someone else's insensitivities when they themselves have the same reputation.

But there is something else to examine here. When we begin to feel someone is inconsiderate, before we confront him, let us pause to ask ourselves, "Is it possible I might be overly sensitive to the slights of others? Am I too easily bruised?"

We cannot control what others do but we can decide whether or not it will affect us. There are times we are convinced someone has wronged us when the other party simply did not do *what* we expected him to do, *when* we expected him to do it. Sometimes we feel we deserve certain treatment and when we don't receive it we wave the insensitive card. Sometimes we just get our feelings hurt.

As much as possible, refuse to be offended. This is a true sign of a fully formed, Christ-follower. Even when someone else is being utterly thoughtless, refuse to take offense. While his actions may be wrong, he may not have a clue of their effect. Choose to think the best. Refuse to react or retaliate.

I decided long ago that I wanted to live a life free of the control of other's poor behavior toward me. This happens when I learn to forgive quickly and purpose not to take offense—even in the Name of Jesus—to words or conduct.

## LEADER IMPERATIVES

Years ago, our church went through a time some lovingly refer to as "The Train Wreck of '95." To help ease the pain of our ordeal I invited anyone who wanted to come to my office to talk with me. My greatest discovery from daily meetings lasting for several months was that my push to accomplish the vision God gave me for the church had become more important than the people themselves. I wanted to justify my task-strong personality. However, God showed me that, while my wiring was no mistake, my actions had to change.

## GOD'S LEADERS ARE NOT BIG SHOTS

"Jesus got them together to settle things down. 'You've observed how god-less rulers throw their weight around,' He said, 'and when people get a little power how quickly it goes to their heads. It's not going to be that way with you. Whoever wants to be great must become a servant.'" (Mark 10:42–43, The Message)

While we are instructed to honor those who lead well among us, God is clear about the heart He wants in a leader of His Church. A Christ-guided leader is humble, not proud, not boastful, nor arrogant. In many ways, a church leader should be the opposite of most leaders we see hallowed in the marketplace and academia.

## GOD'S LEADERS MUST SHOW COMPASSION

"When He saw the crowds, He had compassion on them, because they were harassed and helpless, like sheep without a shepherd." (Matthew 9:36, NIV)

When Jesus saw people, He did not identify a vulnerable group ripe for domination, but lost souls longing for empathy and direction, and it moved Him. What is in our heart will determine if we see people with compassion or condemnation, grace or guilt, even love or loathing.

God, give us Your heart!

Give us Your eyes!

## SENSITIVITY TO DIE FOR

Though I have pulled this card more than once, let me say it again: Jesus never justified a lapse in sensitivity due to a heavy workload. He challenges me with His personal power to sense the feelings of those around Him. And what stuns me most is His ability to do this even in the moment of His most intense agony.

"But the other criminal rebuked him. 'Don't you fear God,' he said, 'since you are under the same sentence? We are punished justly, for we are getting what our deeds deserve. But this man has done nothing wrong.' Then he said, 'Jesus, remember me when You come into Your kingdom.' Jesus answered him, 'I tell you the truth, today you will be with Me in paradise.'" (Luke 23:40–43, NIV)

May we as leaders not be so driven by the mission that we miss the pained look on a face. May we model our management styles after Jesus. And may we as followers lovingly forgive and guide our leaders to a "more excellent way" when they fail.

# BELIEVER INSENSITIVITIES

## CHAPTER FIFTEEN: *Francis Anfuso*

"Nobody knows the trouble I've seen. Nobody knows my sorrow." This old spiritual laments with woeful melody and heartbreaking lyrics how many of us have felt.

I will never forget a six-month period when I was a young, despondent atheist. If I focus on the memory, I can still taste the emotion. I contemplated suicide every day, convinced I was broken beyond repair.

Who can know the depth of a person's pain? Who, but God! He alone has been with us, especially during the most heart-wrenching moments of our lives. He saw the injustice. He heard the hurtful words. He loved us through every poor decision. "Nobody knows the trouble I've seen. Nobody knows but Jesus." The facts are in: only God can fix the unfixable.

And we can be a tool in His toolbox as He wields repair.

- We can be *His eyes*—embracing pain with complete empathy, weeping with those who weep.

- We can be *His ears*—listening with rapt attention as a heart breaks open, pouring out what has been hidden far too long and hurts way too deep.

- We can be *His hands*—touching in a way that says, "I may not know exactly how you feel, but I know Someone who does and loves you dearly. As He has helped me, He will help you."

We are not only Christ's body, but also the only visible representation of His heart to this broken planet. We were created to reveal His tenderness, to demonstrate His compassion and to extend His kindness to a disbelieving world.

## JUST A LITTLE MORE LOVE

We long for *perfect*—to see it…even to be it. But an ocean of imperfection surrounds us. We fall short…far short. Yet, perfect is still what we thirst for: perfect peace, perfect hope, and perfect love.

We disdain imperfection in others and even ourselves. Is this a longing to break free from self-obsession to the higher ground of selfless love?

Perfect can only be found in the heart of a perfect God.

One survey participant who had experienced both leader and believer insensitivities wrote, "I have intentionally chosen not to be offended and bitter. Instead of waiting to be accepted, I look for those who need to be loved and accepted. Also I think the Lord planned for me to get what I felt I needed from Him, not from others. It caused me to search Him more."

The higher ground for this believer had not always been so clear. For a season, these insensitivities fueled her thoughts of abandoning church and Christianity altogether. Describing in detail these hurtful retorts, she related how, "At the time, I just needed people to come around me, not coddle me, but hear what I had been through and pray with me. A lot of it was very intense and hard to deal with. I was more or less told to get over and move past it."

This reminds me of many occasions in the early years of my marriage to Suzie. My wife wanted to be heard. I wanted to fix her. God wanted to use me for this purpose through patient listening. It's amazing how well the Holy Spirit is able to do a healing work through us, when we listen sensitively.

But a sensitive world is not the world we live in.

We must learn to respond well when confronted with the inevitable insensitivities of life. The young woman above didn't pull out of her discouragement overnight, nor did the world change around her. In the end, her own good choices, not the poor choices of others, were the difference-maker in her life, as they can be in ours.

The Bible confirms this "hide and seek" relationship with God. "It is the glory of God to conceal a matter, but the glory of kings is to search out a matter." (Proverbs 25:2, NKJV) God's unshakeable promise to each of us is, "And you will seek Me and find Me, when you search for Me with all your heart." (Jeremiah 29:13, NKJV)

Though we fail daily, His Word remains faithful every moment!

After God led the woman to a healthy church she wrote, "I wasn't trusting of leaders or any kind of authority. I now can trust the leaders that God has placed in my life and I respect them. I love attending a church where everyone is encouraged to be transparent and seek wholeness—this is represented by our leaders."

According to her confession, she is now completely healed.

The healing we seek creates hunger. Not just a craving that fixates on self, but an insatiable passion to help others. Our own longing for healing emboldens us to prepare a caring feast for souls needing to be loved or understood. Somewhere up around a few more healthy bends in the road, a famished soul is waiting for you. You are presently being equipped to demonstrate to them that God can and does heal.

Believe it! You are becoming the healing others long to receive. Embracing this concept will help you fully commit to the many stretching dimensions of the healing process.

## BENEVOLENT BELIEVERS

Though a leader may be graced with a gift of communication, he or she may lack the compassion found so abundant in the heart of a fellow believer. At times, all is lost until compassion is found.

A battered wife wrote, "After leaving my emotionally, spiritually, and borderline physically abusive husband (I had left him after he had a loaded gun in one of his rages with me, and it was one of many times) I was told by my church counselor that I needed to stay with [my husband] and pray more, regardless of the threat of my life. I've heard from both Christian leaders and believers, that divorce is not an option, and that since I did decide to proceed with divorce that I should never remarry. It has all been very hurtful and confusing."

In the *Church Wounds Survey* she further added how her gradual break-through came through trusting in God's Word. "Every time I went to the Word, I read of God's love and faithfulness, and about His promises to prosper me with a hope and a future. I began to be concerned about how God unconditionally felt about me. It still is hard to get past some of the stuff they said though, and their judgments."

God gave her a poignant verse to hold on to: "the One who formed you says, 'Do not be afraid, for I have ransomed you. I have called you by name; you are Mine. When you go through deep waters, I will be with you. When you go through rivers of difficulty, you will not drown. When you walk through the fire of oppression, you will not be burned up; the flames will not consume you. For I am the Lord, your God, the Holy One of Israel, your Savior…because you are precious to Me. You are honored, and I love you.'" (Isaiah 43:1–2, 3a, 4b)

Another woman wrote, after a breakthrough from past church wounds, "Understanding Jesus as my model of and motivation for forgiveness, I can forgive. I also realize that most of the time none of the wounds were intentional; the church is full of people just like me. I need to have realistic expectations. God has enabled me to forgive nearly all hurts and offenses. I do still carry some resentment toward one individual and continue to work on giving it to God, letting it go into His hands when it comes to mind. He has taught me to freely give the grace I want to receive from others; to let go of offenses quickly; to stay humble."

### THE CURE FOR INSENSITIVITY

Though leader insensitivities were listed as the 2nd most prevalent cause of church wounds (noted on 40 percent of all surveys), believer insensitivities were relegated to the 23rd spot (noted on a mere 15 percent of the surveys). In some cases, the one-two punch of combined leader and believer insensitivities knocked people out of fellowship altogether.

A thirty-something woman who took our *Church Wounds Survey* spoke of her catastrophic struggles. She was so traumatized by the insensitivities of both leaders and believers she wrote, "The most hurtful to me were insensitivities when I needed help the most. I felt lost and actually went down a terrible path in response to it. I left my marriage, church and God behind."

Broken and depressed, she walked away from God for seven years.

As believer insensitivities played a part in her moving away from God, so a caring, non-judgmental Christ-like atmosphere was a major contributing factor drawing this woman back to a healthy relationship with Jesus and His people. She further confided, "The most helpful to me was when I came to a healthy church. I felt I had finally found a place that wasn't going to judge me for my past. I was able to find a place where I could be me—wounds and all. This allowed me to open up to God's healing and allow Him to free me from my past."

She continued to describe her healing journey, "I need to always run to the Lord immediately if I am feeling wounded." How effective was this woman's pursuit of freedom from the demons of past insensitivities? Apparently, very! She expressed her elation at the victory God had provided, "For the first time I feel like I can be real with people and not worry about their judgments."

Can an eminently sensitive God meet our need to be understood? Is this possible, even if people miss the mark? Absolutely! New generations of authentic ambassadors of God's heart are being raised up, groomed to model God's sensitive response to chronic insensitivity.

Here again, God's Word provides a clear roadmap for living—how to avoid hurting others. "Let each of you look out not only for his own interests, but also for the interests of others." (Philippians 2:4, NKJV)

Paul the Apostle further expressed God's heart, "Each one of us needs to look after the good of the people around us, asking ourselves, 'How can I help?'" (Romans 15:2, The Message) You know you're thinking God thoughts when you're focused on the needs of others over your own.

The Bible provides a clear path to developing this Christ-like mindset. "And we urge you, brothers and sisters, admonish the undisciplined, comfort the discouraged, help the weak, be patient toward all." (1 Thessalonians 5:14, NET)

When the Bible speaks of *comforting the discouraged,* it specifically means those whose hearts are faint or afraid. *Helping the weak* refers to holding fast and supporting those who are more feeble, impotent, sick, or without strength.

All around us, people are plagued by tormenting sins. While vigilance is needed to resist temptation, acknowledging weakness enables us to empathize with the struggle in others. God wants to use us to help others overcome consistently weak areas. "Stoop down and reach out to those who are oppressed. Share their burdens, and so complete Christ's law." (Galatians 6:2, The Message)

As Jesus ever lives to stoop down and reach out to us (Hebrews 7:25), may we in turn receive a daily infusion of His heart for those who have lost theirs.

# MISUSE OF SPIRITUAL GIFTS

## CHAPTER SIXTEEN (PART A): *David Loveless*

Some years ago I sat with anticipation on the front row at a Sunday morning service awaiting a message from a guest speaker. I had heard of significant, if not unusual, experiences occurring in God's presence at his church. I invited him to our church hoping we might be encouraged to deepen our relationships with Jesus. But for many, what happened was far from uplifting. Like a bullet train that jumps the tracks and lunges for a crowd of bystanders, the devastation unfolded as I watched, paralyzed.

As the pastor paced the stage telling his story, he announced the Holy Spirit was about to do some unusual things, manifest Himself in ways some might not be used to, but we were not to worry, God was in the House. God was in control.

Then the pastor chose random people to join him on stage. Almost as fast as they got there these people fell to the floor "under the power of God." One of them began to scream while another laughed hysterically. Then some in their seats erupted in similar behavior, expressions most would consider cause for calling mental health professionals. Stunned, scared, and bewildered, several hundred people left before the service was over. Most of them never returned.

Throughout this scene I sat pinned in my seat puzzled. Were we witnessing a supernatural, authentic move of the Holy Spirit, or a cataclysmic attack on our church? Some scriptures warn us not to quench the Spirit while others define order in worship. Which ones applied here? Was this a true move of God or a flamboyant attempt to incite emotion? Afterward a few seemed genuinely helped but the majority were dazed, confused, and most definitely divided. I think I have come to believe that the greatest act of God that day was that our church sustained a train wreck. We were battered and bloodied yet somehow still breathing.

After this we had some pretty dirty bathwater to toss out. But the question remained, how do we not lose our grip of the 'baby'?

The Bible teaches and demonstrates the beauty, power, healing, and encouragement of individuals and churches, using the gifts of the Holy Spirit.

I am thinking of a service recently where we saw God affect many people in redeeming ways. The difference between this weekend and what we now lovingly refer to as the "train wreck of '95", is that this time God's presence affected lives without fear, confusion or the alienation of an entire congregation and inquiring guests.

Countless people have been wounded in and around the church, through the misappropriation of gifts. While many feel only a few gifts are prone to abuse, after 30 years of vocational ministry, I believe any one of them has the potential to be misused, mishandled or mismanaged in some way.

When we read the passages listing the gifts and manifestations of the Holy Spirit it seems all of them could be helpful depending on the need (Romans 12, 1Corinthians 12). However, any one of them, in the wrong hands with the wrong motivation, may wreck havoc in people's lives, disorienting them from the true, holy purposes of the church, leaving some in spiritual posttraumatic shock for life.

After listing God's distribution of these gifts in 1Corinthians 12, the Apostle Paul introduces the grand theme of 1Corinthians 13 by saying, "And now I will show you the most excellent way."

I would guess that 1Corinthians 13 has been quoted at more weddings than all other scripture combined. Nothing could be more lovely, entreating, or desirable than this kind of love. But hang on a moment. 1Corinthians 13 was not written for wedding ceremonies. This magnificent chapter was penned to correct the abuse of spiritual gifts in the church. Apparently the situation was in such shambles Paul needed three chapters in his first letter to the church at Corinth to sort it all out for them.

## DISORDERLY CONDUCT

Years ago, conference speakers, identified as prophets, declared futuristic events in people's lives, completely mesmerizing a man I knew. One of the prophets predicted many things about this man's job and leadership potential. For several decades he used the prophet's words like yard sticks for measuring significant decisions. Many years later, I discovered he was still interpreting his life's work through what he believed to be the infallible words God spoke through that prophet, even though many who knew him well and observed his life could not validate the accuracy of the prophet's words.

Once I was asked to teach at a conference where, at the end of his talk, one speaker invited several leaders to stand at the front. The speaker then began to yell and rant streams of words he alleged were from God specifically for those leaders. I watched in horror as his aggression rose to the point of physically pushing the men around, ultimately to the ground, shouting that his strange behavior was to be seen as the power of God, seeking to 'hit them.'

Recently, a so-called spiritual awakening, happening in a city not far from where I live, grabbed national attention. The news of this revival spread so far and wide that I was asked about it while traveling in other countries. Truly interested in any real move of God I pulled up a video of one of the pastor's services on the Internet. I saw a woman in front of the preacher kneeling in prayer ready to receive a benevolent touch from God when suddenly the man kicked her and, in a booming voice, roared that sometimes God does violent things to unleash his power and get our attention.

The statements of spiritual carnage from that particular "move of God" still come in as we write this book.

While many less observable abuses have transpired, these three scenarios are blatantly obvious:

- Someone is teaching God's Word, either in a small or large group, and uses scripture to accomplish his or her own agenda or to manipulate people to act in some way.

- A person claiming the gift of faith uses it to convince others to do something foolish that God has not confirmed.
- Someone with the gift of helps uses it to make other people, who do not possess that gift, feel guilty for not serving in the same selfless manner.

## PUTTING GIFTS IN THEIR PLACE

The multiple purposes for the use of spiritual gifts include:

- Glorify God
- Build faith in God
- Manifest the supernatural character of Christ's Church to the world
- Offer spiritual deliverance
- Provide personal or congregational encouragement, comfort and assurance
- Encourage a heightened sense of warning, caution, insight and direction
- Bring to full maturity the perfecting of the saints in the Body of Christ

## BEST USE OF GIFTS

Always subject to scripture, exercising spiritual gifts, under any condition, must complement and never contradict other primary teachings of God's Word. When observing or employing spiritual gifts apply these clarifying questions:

1.  *Is the public use of the gift in subjection to the elders of a local church?*

    The Bible teaches that God places part of His authority in human leaders within the church. Spiritual leaders, in turn, discern the legitimacy as well as the timing of the use of gifts.

"The spirits of prophets are subject to the control of prophets. For God is not a God of disorder but of peace." (1Corinthians 14:22, NIV)

2. *Is the gift exercised with and motivated by the love of Christ?*

Scripture clearly explicates, whenever using any type of gift, the primary goal should be a love for God and one another.

"If I speak in the tongues of men and of angels, but have not love, I am only a resounding gong or a clanging cymbal. If I have the gift of prophecy and can fathom all mysteries and all knowledge, and if I have a faith that can move mountains, but have not love, I am nothing. If I give all I possess to the poor and surrender my body to the flames but have not love, I gain nothing." (1Corinthians 13:1–3, NIV)

3. *Does the gift build up the gathered people into more fully devoted followers of Christ or does it seek to build up itself?*

Our attitude toward gifts must be selfless. There is no room to use God's gifts to draw attention, gain something, or demonstrate personal piety. These gifts must glorify God and strengthen His church.

"Since you are eager to have spiritual gifts, try to excel in gifts that build up the church." (1Corinthians 14:12, NIV)

4. *Is the gift yielded to God in a spirit of self-control?*

A few years ago, two people, in a period of six months, interrupted my message at a weekend service by shouting a word they believed was from God.

In both incidences I waited until they took a breath and said: "I appreciate that you feel you have a Word from God for this church. However, I was in the middle of sharing the word God has given me, and you disrupted me. Please sit quietly until after the service then myself and other pastors will be glad to listen to what you have to say."

In one case, a woman sat down. In the other case, the person continued to shout and the ushers gently removed him. When several pastors talked with the person in the lobby, he said he could not control himself because he was overcome by God.

It is astounding that God wants to operate through us at all by the way we act sometimes! The fact that He pours His spirit on us and invites us to engage in a Kingdom partnership with Him is stunning. When He does use us, it is a cooperative act. We have not been employed as a robot. We seek to align ourselves with God's intentions and obey in a way that best represents Him. This takes great spiritual maturity and discernment, especially if exercised in the context of the larger body of Christ.

Someone expressing a spiritual gift should not be abusive or emotionally deranged saying he cannot control himself, "the Holy Spirit made him do it." If someone distracts a meeting by screaming a prophecy, shaking or laughing, or other extremes that do not edify the body but produces confusion, disorder and/or fear, his actions must be gently addressed.

**IF YOU'VE BEEN WOUNDED BY THE MISUSE OF SPIRITUAL GIFTS:**

- Realize that the misuse of something doesn't negate its legitimacy when used properly. The misuse of a medical procedure does not negate the need for it. Do not allow yourself to become cynical or faithless. There can only be a counterfeit of something that already genuinely exists.

- Realize that some people, in their initial zeal to use their gifts, sometimes do not demonstrate needful wisdom. Forgive them, for they are not fully mature in Christ. A car in the hands of a student driver or a substance abuser is potentially more dangerous than one operated by a seasoned vehicle veteran.

- Find a church that believes in the gifts of the spirit, but practices those gifts within the guidelines provided above.

- If you see someone regularly abusing any of the gifts and you have some relationship to or responsibility for them, talk with them. Otherwise alert a wise church leader with your concerns but do not gossip.

When I think of the best ways to demonstrate all the gifts I always look to Jesus. "Jesus, full of the Holy Spirit, returned from the Jordan and was led by the Spirit." (Luke 4:1, NIV)

Who was more empowered or filled with the Holy Spirit than Jesus? Yet when we see him teaching or healing we see Him do so with humility acting only on what was needed in that moment. When He turned water into wine, He did not make it rain wine for 40 days and 40 nights. When He healed a leper He did not alert the entire town to form a prayer line and take up a half-hour offering.

Yes, I have seen and experienced spiritual gifts in the hands of questionables, and have been grieved for their tarnish and defamation of the true glory of God. But I have witnessed even more gifts exercised by godly men and women who represent Him well.

One such person is Francis Anfuso, my close friend and co-author. He has been a powerful example to me and countless other leaders over the years in this area. I have watched him seek to employ clearly needed spiritual gifts in a moment. Both church services and private gatherings have witnessed his humble, gentle, ways before the Lord and the leadership. Each time he denounces the personal spotlight in order to minister with genuine compassion.

This is the goal of true spiritual gifts and the most God-honoring way to release the supernatural presence of the Living God. When we use wisdom and discernment in the power of love we ordinary humans can help one another grow up into to all the fullness Christ.

Consider this. Even under the power of the Holy Spirit Jesus committed no violence as He ministered to people's needs. He lived a life of non-violence. Yes, He turned over some tables once to make a point. (No animals or children were harmed in the making of that point either.) And He once made mention that the violent would take the kingdom by force. Though He easily could have, Jesus refused to align himself with the zealots of His day and never fought in His own defense. Perhaps the oddest thing He ever did during a healing was to put mud over a blind man's eyes. Conversely, when the enemy outs himself, violence and screaming are standard practice. If gentleness and self-control evidence the Holy Spirit's presence (Galatians 5), it does not seem likely He would contradict Himself by displaying his gifts through physical aggression.

# MISUSE OF SPIRITUAL GIFTS

## CHAPTER SIXTEEN (PART B): *Francis Anfuso*

For myself, I found it difficult to discern God's voice the first nine years of my Christian life. In 1981, the Spirit of God spoke to my heart, not audibly, but clearly, that He was going to teach me to hear His voice so that I could in turn teach others. I then spent the next few years fasting, praying and studying scripture extensively, even writing a lengthy textbook on the subject.

From 1984 through 1997, I traveled throughout the Body of Christ ministering to over 16,000 individual people in the gifts of the Spirit. Hour after hour, night after night, year after year, I poured myself into hearing and obeying God. It was a sacred trust. Though the level of accuracy was very high, it was not flawless. Many a time, I agonized over situations that turned out less than I had hoped.

I even contemplated never again stepping out in the gifts of Spirit if I could not see 100% accuracy, accompanied by greater power and anointing. Over time, the Spirit of God encouraged me that my imperfection in ministry was intended to keep me humble and fully dependent upon Him. Jesus appropriately noted, "…apart from Me you can do nothing." (John 15:5)

Many times, I went to sleep on cloud nine, having soared in the spirit realm, and overjoyed at what the Lord had done. But, on more occasions then I care to remember I would drift off to sleep glad the uncertainties of the evening were over, and entrusting into God's gracious hands all I had attempted to do on His behalf.

Ministering in the gifts of the Spirit is not an exact science.

It is not for the faint of heart. But, it is certainly worth it.

After spending many hours ministering over scores of people in a large church, one pastor told me my ministry in the gifts of Spirit was surprisingly conservative. I'm not sure he meant it completely as a positive comment, but I received it as such. I had read and seen enough of the damage done to the name of Jesus and the people of God throughout church history that I did not want to add to the carnage. Perhaps these concerns caused me to miss some divine opportunities, but in retrospect I am honored that so many lives were touched.

Even now, many years later, I still receive near-weekly emails from people whose lives were positively impacted during those years of extensive travel and ministry in the gifts of Spirit. I am eternally grateful that this legacy of ministry was far more constructive than confusing. To God alone be the glory!

### MIXED FRUIT

At times, when I sat under the anointed ministry of others in the Body of Christ, my experience was more of a mixed bag, running the gamut from amazed to annoyed, blessed to bewildered. I rejoiced in the transformed lives, healed bodies, and stellar testimonies of God's power and grace. But over time, I became equally troubled by the lack of character amongst leaders, the emotional frenzy experiential manifestations promoted, and the lack of ability to discern the clear boundaries of the Spirit's anointing. I wasn't alone. Fourteen percent of those who took our *Church Wounds Survey* said they were wounded by the misuse of the gifts of the Spirit.

We all long to see God move in an authentic, life-transforming way. But we need to make sure it is God who is moving, and not us. In addition, however we catch them, will be how we keep them! The bait we use will make all of the difference. Unless we model complete dependency upon God's Spirit, and not man's charisma and manipulation, swirling signs and wonders, and unusually visitations, we will be merely dancing on the altar long after the sacrifice has been consumed. God doesn't need us to prop Him up. He needs our surrendered, yielded hearts.

In my own experience of ministering in the gifts of the Spirit, I found that my number one stewardship was not to "do something," but rather to "do nothing." Unless God could trust me to "do nothing without Him," He was unable to trust me to "do something with Him". This fully submitted perspective was tested on many occasions. Would I accept the humiliation of doing nothing while waiting upon God to move? Or, would I draw from my remembrance of past experiences, and create a pseudo-spiritual atmosphere? This is always the great test. "Test all things; hold fast what is good." (1Thessalonians 5:21, NKJV)

Like David Loveless' firsthand experience, I, at times, witnessed the residue of confusion left in the wake of a seeming move of God. Only God knows what really happened. But, if we are to judge the fruit as Jesus asked us to, then mixed fruit was at best what took place. I'm not saying that each of us will not at times find that what we have harvested was "mixed fruit," but I would say our willingness to acknowledge both our good and bad fruit will determine the extent we have been obedient to the Lord's will for our lives.

## UNQUESTIONABLE FRUIT

Suzie and I are eternally grateful for the supernatural impartation we witnessed first-hand in the lives of our daughters Deborah and Havilah. During a genuine move of God in their teenage years, they were dramatically touched and transformed by His Spirit. Were there unusual manifestations? Yes, many more than we were comfortable with. Did their experiences defy our understanding? Without a doubt! Did it leave an impartation that was life-altering? Absolutely! Was guidance needed to protect them from being enamored by the external, and focused on God's Word and His life-transforming grace? It became our number one priority.

So, a genuine move of God, like any harvest, will require the removal of weeds—the chaff from the wheat. What is eternal, from the temporal distractions of Earth? This is the great test! Will we embrace the good, while discerning the bad? Or will we throw up our hands in frustration saying, "It's too complicated! I'll settle for what I can fully understand." If we bow to this lesser god, we will certainly miss divine appointments that would have made all the difference. We know this was the case for our daughters.

I don't want to miss God.

Nor do I want to misrepresent Him.

Only by daily leaning upon Him will I see both.

# CONTROLLING SPIRIT

*Section Five*

# PRIDE

## CHAPTER SEVENTEEN: *David Loveless*

"In a church I used to attend," a woman in her 40s said in our *Church Wounds Survey*, "the minister received an exorbitant salary while bills for the church went unpaid. There was no church budget or… accountability. This pastor was never wrong and would not listen to others. When approached with questions about his conduct he became verbally abusive and grossly misused scripture. Even though I've moved on it bothers me this person is still in ministry and I have a great deal of anger over the injustice of it all. Of the many families that left that church the vast majority of marriages are wrecked and children are in trouble. Though everyone is responsible for his or her own actions I believe the impact of the leadership of that church was a factor. Lack of humility in leaders really concerns me."

Some time ago I sat in a meeting listening to the details of an encounter where one person had offended several others. The offended ones had tried to talk through the situation on their own but to no avail and all were now seeking my counsel. Throughout the conversation, this person responded to the charges against him by saying, "I don't know what you are talking about. This is their problem, not mine. I don't do such things."

As I listened to the denials I kept thinking, "If you just admit your mistake, own it and confess it, then you can learn from it and move on." But the person would not be humbled; he would not yield his position and refused to see any error.

Pride is an ugly, destructive attitude. The culprit behind untold numbers of rifts, it destroys relationships between spouses, co-workers, partners and life-long friends. Sadly, the church must also be included as a victim of devastation at the hands of stubborn, prideful people.

Biblical warnings of a proud heart render us unexcused.

## PRIDE 101

*When pride comes, then comes disgrace, but with humility comes wisdom.*
*(Proverbs 11:2, NIV)*

*Pride only breeds quarrels, but wisdom is found in those who take advice.*
*(Proverbs 13:10, NIV)*

*Pride goes before destruction, a haughty spirit before a fall.*
*(Proverbs 16:18, NIV)*

The narrative of 2 Chronicles provides an image of pride and its injury.
Hezekiah led the children of Israel and accomplished much. He con-
structed agricultural villages and built storage facilities for the people; he
also helped reroute the primary water supply during a time of war, in a very
creative fashion, to prevent death from thirst. Then Hezekiah became ill.

*So the LORD saved Hezekiah and the people of Jerusalem from the hand of*
*Sennacherib king of Assyria and from the hand of all others. He took care of*
*them on every side. Many brought offerings to Jerusalem for the LORD and valu-*
*able gifts for Hezekiah king of Judah. From then on he was highly regarded by all*
*the nations. In those days Hezekiah became ill and was at the point of death. He*
*prayed to the LORD, who answered him and gave him a miraculous sign. But*
*Hezekiah's heart was proud and he did not respond to the kindness shown him;*
*therefore the LORD's wrath was on him and on Judah and Jerusalem. Then*
*Hezekiah repented of the pride of his heart, as did the people of Jerusalem;*
*therefore the LORD's wrath did not come upon them during the days of*
*Hezekiah. (2Chronicles 32:22–26, NIV)*

When good things happen, when accomplishments are achieved, we
have to decide if we will share recognition with the team or claim the
credit alone.

Not long ago, representatives from a national company met with a group
from our church to determine if they would help us refinance our church's
mortgage. After hours of examination and interviews they saw huge
changes and financial advances we had made. One of them said: "We have
been doing this for 19 years and have never seen such a successful budget
turnaround." They went on to make several other complimentary remarks
about us.

In that moment, I had several options. I could react as if I was responsible for this outcome. Or I could say, "Thank you so much. As you can imagine, it has taken a great deal of hard work to get us here. Much of the success of this turnaround is because of these other incredible folks and a team of people they represent."

I chose the high road but not because I am always a humble servant leader. I am sorry to say there have been more than a few times I needed someone else to lovingly help me see a more complete picture to our success. The memory of those chastening remarks still stings. God uses them to encourage me toward the goal of the humble leader I truly desire to be.

What happened at the end of that meeting was both interesting and heartening. After watching our leaders interact, the CEO of this firm commented on the unusual atmosphere of listening, authenticity, and humility among the church headship. He especially noted that they admit mistakes and seek to learn from each other.

Now that was something to be proud of.

### NATIONAL PRIDE

Once an entire country was severely chastised for its arrogance. Through the prophet Jeremiah the Lord says, "'Moab's horn is cut off; her arm is broken,' declares the LORD. 'Make her drunk, for she has defied the LORD. Let Moab wallow in her vomit; let her be an object of ridicule. Abandon your towns and dwell among the rocks, you who live in Moab. Be like a dove that makes its nest at the mouth of a cave. We have heard of Moab's pride—her overweening pride and conceit, her pride and arrogance and the haughtiness of her heart. I know her insolence but it is futile,' declares the LORD, 'and her boasts accomplish nothing.'" (Jeremiah 48:25–30, NIV)

The country of Moab was east of the Dead Sea. Jeremiah paints a picture of impending destruction. There was going to be a wounding on a massive scale. God said that Moab's physical security and history of relative peace had led her to become arrogant.

A king was cited in scripture for a similar sin.

In Daniel chapters four and five, we read of Nebuchadnezzar, king of the Babylonian Empire. The most powerful monarch of his time, well known for the size and beauty of Babylon's capital, he ruled the largest city of the world. Nebuchadnezzar was also known for his many military victories. So, on top of his skill as a warlord, he was also adept at politics. Among other nations, Nebuchadnezzar defeated Judah. Daniel describes the looting of Jerusalem and the captivity of the Hebrews in Babylon.

But as King Nebuchadnezzar grew in power, the Bible says he also amassed an arsenal of pride that literally devastated vast numbers of people. God punishes the king for this great sin and uses his life as a lesson for us.

> *O king, the Most High God gave your father Nebuchadnezzar sovereignty and greatness and glory and splendor. Because of the high position he gave him, all the peoples and nations and men of every language dreaded and feared him. Those the king wanted to put to death, he put to death; those he wanted to spare, he spared; those he wanted to promote, he promoted; and those he wanted to humble, he humbled. But when his heart became arrogant and hardened with pride, he was deposed from his royal throne and stripped of his glory. He was driven away from people and given the mind of an animal; he lived with the wild donkeys and ate grass like cattle; and his body was drenched with the dew of heaven, until he acknowledged that the Most High God is sovereign over the kingdoms of men and sets over them anyone he wishes. (Daniel 5:18–21)*

The Bible says that there are only a few things that God literally hates. Pride is one of them. "To fear the LORD is to hate evil; I hate pride and arrogance." (Proverbs 8:13)

God drove Nebuchadnezzar from the people and made him live with the animals in the field! He literally roamed the land, eating grass for seven years. This entire mind-numbing activity ceased when he eventually humbled himself and acknowledged God as King of the heaven.

*At the same time that my sanity was restored, my honor and splendor were returned to me for the glory of my kingdom. My advisers and nobles sought me out, and I was restored to my throne and became even greater than before. Now I, Nebuchadnezzar, praise and exalt and glorify the King of heaven, because everything he does is right and all his ways are just. And those who walk in pride he is able to humble. (Daniel 4:36–37)*

The Babylonian kingdom was later destroyed as had been revealed to Daniel in a vision.

Now here's something I find fascinating. If a world-wide poll were taken and people were asked to name the top five most prideful leaders of the 20th century, one of those would probably be Saddam Hussein. This 20th century ruler over Iraq (former Babylon) literally considered himself to be the reincarnation of Nebuchadnezzar. The inscription, "To King Nebuchadnezzar in the reign of Saddam Hussein," was emblazoned on multitudes of bricks comprising the ancient walls during the reconstruction that Hussein initiated. And like Nebuchadnezzar, Saddam's pride in his accomplishments contributed to his downfall.

### PRIDE WOUNDS WHEN

- Someone takes the credit where others have clearly contributed. It hurts when we have worked, conceptualized and sacrificed without being acknowledged. It hurts when those who have clearly added value do not receive appreciation.

- A person refuses to admit he has made a mistake. Like scalding water, it hurts when, though it is clear to everyone else, the person responsible for a poor decision, direction or word cannot admit it.

- A leader doesn't ask other's opinions. It hurts when others know God has given them wisdom for specific things a group or church is facing, but the leader doesn't acknowledge he or she needs additional insight.

- People seek glory for themselves. It hurts when someone must accomplish his own agenda at the expense of a serving soul.

**HEALTHY CHURCHES ARE THOSE WHERE:**

- People share credit with others. Statements like these are common: "I want to thank the following people:_____. And I want to mention the specific things they have contributed:_____. Without these contributions we would not be where we are today. I am honored to know and share the load with these people."

- People admit their mistakes. It is not strange to hear: "After looking at all of the factors that have led to our situation I see how I am responsible for some of what has happened. I certainly did not intend to mess up, but I see I made mistakes. Please forgive me for these things. I have learned valuable lessons and would like the opportunity to apply them while moving forward."

- Christ-followers give glory to God, seeking to make Him famous. "I am humbled that you and I have had this opportunity to play a small role in this amazing thing God accomplished here. This clearly could not have happened apart from the amazing power and love of God."

- Leaders listen to others and make adjustments along the way saying things like: "I have some important decisions to make and I know that I don't see the whole picture, just parts of it. I am in great need of your eyes and insight. No one has it all together, but together we have it all. I want to hear what you think and sense God is saying to us."

**WHEN PRIDE IS PAINFUL TO WATCH:**

- Commit to pray for those involved including yourself and your response to them. Ask God to reveal to them their pride and to have mercy as He brings them to repentance.

- Ask God to show you pride and "the log" that is potentially in your own life. Ask what may be contributing toward the escalation of your hard-heartedness.

- Sit down with a leader and talk with him if he seems unaware of his chronic pride that is hurting you or others. Provide him with specific examples. Tell him that you believe this does not represent the best version of who you know him to be.

- Forgive. Forgive. Forgive.

The challenge to live in humility before the Lord and others is a God-worthy goal and, also, a never-ending challenge.

Even as I write this chapter I am reminded of a recent breakfast with one of our leaders. As happens sometimes, in the trenches of ministry, the two of us had been through a rough patch and I wanted to be sure we were good with each other relationally.

So I asked my friend if there was anything I had done to contribute to the intense exchange between us in some meetings. He looked at me and said, "David, sometimes you get defensive when people try to give you honest feedback."

Now there was more to this conversation but suffice it to say it did not feel all that great to receive his honesty. I sat there as calm as I could but I still felt pride rear its ugly head for about the 39,000th time in my life. I so much wanted to say, "Now, come on, I don't do that!" At that moment, I did want to defend myself (the very fault being exposed); more important I wanted to be understood and just a little appreciated for the times I had welcomed his comments and advice. I wanted to ask if he thought *he* had ever been defensive.

But I held steady.

After listening for a few minutes I simply expressed appreciation for his desire to help me be the best pastor I can be. I solicited his ongoing prayers for me as I continue to grow on the path to humility.

Yeah, still got a ways to go yet.

If you think of it, you can pray for me too.

# JUDGEMENTALISM

## CHAPTER EIGHTEEN: *David Loveless*

As I write this chapter, I am sitting on a plane in first class. My legs are stretched out, my computer's propped open and the flight attendant has just taken the order for my beverage of choice. Now before you get worked up with thoughts like, "I wonder who paid for his ticket? Isn't that a waste of good Kingdom money? Wouldn't Jesus be riding in coach?" you should know it cost me nothing to sit here. I travel so much with this airline, it sometimes upgrades me from coach to first class for free. But if you did not know this I wonder what might go through *your* mind today if you had boarded the same plane and spotted me here on your way to the cheap seats?

### JUDGMENT CALLS

It happens everyday to all of us. Snap judgments. Someone appears in a better or lesser place than us and we make certain assessments about why this should or should not be. Maybe someone is doing something, saying something, wearing something we disapprove of and we feel an inner compulsion to either correct her thinking or assign her to some category beneath us. Where does this come from? How, after all Jesus did to teach us otherwise, does condescension and spiritual snobbery still stalk the halls of the 21st century church?

Two stories from our *Church Wounds Survey* show how far off the mark the Church still is in this area.

A father said, *While raising our children we felt strongly we should put them in public school so they could learn to be in the world but not of it. We wanted to disciple them to be missionaries within their classrooms, sports teams and network of friends. But the small church we attended was made up of mostly home schooling families who constantly judged us for putting our kids in school. They relentlessly talked about how evil and terrible public schools were. It got so bad our kids begged us to find another church.*

A woman in her 50's said, *My father was a leader in a fundamentalist church. He was prideful, judgmental and controlled me through guilt. To him our church was right and everyone else was wrong. Then we moved churches and only the new church was right. If I didn't obey he said I was going to hell and God would punish me. I searched for love in the church but most seemed to be judgmental hypocrites. When my son was killed at age 21, the minister preached a fearful, fire and brimstone sermon at his funeral scaring everyone instead of kindly and compassionately reaching out to all the lost kids who listened. What a lost opportunity!*

Where these people could have received healing, the judgmental church threw stones. I have had a few stones hurled my way as well.

### NO SHOES, NO SHIRT, NO SERVICE

In the mid-70s I started a Bible study in my dorm room at the University of South Florida. I was making my own comeback to Jesus at the time and felt burdened to help many of my longhaired, spaced out, hippie friends. Some pretty interesting looking characters showed up and God met us in profound ways. Many of them gave their lives to Christ. One day I suggested we start going to church.

Big mistake.

Instead of grace and mercy we were met with glares, stares and comments of disapproving disgust. I felt angry and devastated. How could I possibly help these folks find God if His church could not receive them? Significant Kingdom points were lost for God's team.

But the Church does not reserve this kind of treatment for outsiders alone, does it? Often we turn on our own, validating the saying, "Christians are the only ones who shoot their wounded."

One mother in our *Church Wounds Survey* affirmed this: "When my daughter became pregnant at age 16, everyone in our church turned their backs on us. Even young children were not allowed to play with my young kids. The church judged our whole family because of our daughter's pregnancy. As a result most of our children have turned away from the church."

Tell the truth. If you had been in this woman's church, how do you think you would have treated her family?

Or how do you respond now when you see others expressing worship in a way that makes you uncomfortable? Does the extra-expressive worshipper distract you with thoughts like, "What in the world is that guy trying to prove?" And if you are one who lifts his hands and waves them in the air or sways to the music or hops or twirls or does Israeli circle dances in the aisle, do you look down on those who are simply singing?

## FIGHT FOR THE LIGHT

Every practice, belief or expression of faith is argued over, wrangled with and called into question by other believers of a slightly different persuasion. In the words of the apostle, "Brethren, these things ought not to be so!" (James 3:10, NKJV)

We must never use the light of God as a *Star Wars* lightsaber to slash someone else. We may have strong convictions about wine, for example, due to personal or family addictions or even because someone we love met death by the wheel of a drunk driver. We may even be convinced we have solid Biblical ground to stand on. Without question we should hold fast to our convictions. But we should cling to them, even champion them as just that—*our convictions*. We are not then free to convict everyone else in our path with a word God gave to us.

As enlightened believers we must lay down all comparisons, measurements and assessments of others. We were never designed to discern the hearts and minds of even those closest to us. So often blind to our own evil, selfish, carnal, prideful, materialistic inclinations, we are unqualified to stand in certain judgment over the actions and attitudes of a co-worker, an acquaintance, or a television personality.

## A GOOD JUDGE OF PEOPLE

In relationships we use our own personality filters for self-protection and self-preservation. We understand the need for healthy boundaries, which sometimes require assessing a person's character as it relates to our own emotional health. At times we may react with natural self-defense instinct if we feel threatened by someone who appears dangerous. But Jesus challenged the Jewish leaders and us to a new relational level when He said in John 7:24, "Stop judging by mere appearances and make a right judgment." (NIV) And long before this, the Lord spoke to the prophet Samuel, "The Lord does not look at the things man looks at. Man looks at the outward appearance, but the Lord looks at the heart." (1Samuel 16:7b, NIV)

Our eyes see in the physical realm only while God has the power to know someone's heart. Yet somehow we make secret judgments of people everyday based on their apparent intellect, economic status, color, gender, class, spiritual maturity, occupation and even their weight. God forgive us!

But isn't there a place for rightly dividing the truth and discerning the presence of evil?

Yes. Though the Bible commands us to love one another, accept one another and bear with the spiritually weak, John, the disciple who knew Jesus loved him, teaches, "Dear friends, do not believe every spirit but test the spirits to see whether they are from God, because many false prophets have gone out into the world." (1John 4:1, NIV)

And how will we spot these false prophets? "This is how you can recognize the Spirit of God. Every spirit that acknowledges that Jesus Christ has come in the flesh is from God, but every spirit that does not acknowledge Jesus is not from God. This is the spirit of the antichrist, which you have heard is coming and even now is already in the world." (1John 4:2, NIV)

In the same chapter of his most quoted sermon, Jesus explained the balance of two foundational principles for His new Kingdom. He said, "Do not judge, or you too will be judged. For in the same way you judge others, you will be judged, and with the measure you use, it will be measured to you. How can you say to your brother, 'Let me take the speck out of your eye, when all the time there is a plank in your own eye?'" (Matthew 7:1–4, NIV)

In the next passage Jesus warns against false prophets whom we will know by the type of fruit they bear. "Every tree that does not bear fruit is cut down and thrown into the fire. By their fruit you will know them. Many will say to me on that day, Lord, Lord did we not prophesy in your name and in your name drive out demons and perform many miracles? Then I will tell them plainly, 'I never knew you. Away from me you evildoers!'" (Matthew 7:19–23, NIV)

First, Jesus admonishes us not to judge one another. Then, to avoid deception, He tells us how to spot a false prophet. Note that Jesus is the one doing the cutting and banishing. Apparently, He can handle this just fine on His own.

### DON'T SWEAT THE SMALL STUFF

One significant aspect of spiritual discernment is learning to distinguish between a non-essential salvation issue, and a core doctrine issue. We learn this discernment by faithfully studying the scriptures and aspiring to the goal Paul gave Timothy to "correctly handle the word of truth." (2Timothy 2:15, NIV)

In Romans 14, Paul says, "Accept him whose faith is weak without passing judgment on disputable matters." He subsequently lists the offenses of the day between Jews and Gentiles. For example, leaders dealt with sacred days for worship and foods and to abstain from drinking. On issues like these, the key, Paul says is, "Each one should be fully convinced in his own mind." (Vs 1, 5, NIV)

Finally, he strongly admonishes us saying, "You then, why do you judge your brother? Or why do you look down on your brother? For we will all stand before God's judgment seat…each of us will give an account of himself to God. Therefore let us stop passing judgment on one another." (Romans 14:10, 12–13, NIV)

Now let's rewind to the beginning of the chapter where I am sitting in first class, comfortable, feet propped up, drink of choice in hand. Suddenly you spot me as you pass by on your way to coach. How do you think you would view that scene now?

## GIVE IT A SECOND THOUGHT

Before you move on, take a few minutes to test your own spirit on this subject. Ask the Holy Spirit to reveal your Christ-less judgments, not upon false prophets or evil spirits but upon your brothers and sisters in Christ. In an honest conversation with Jesus ask:

- As I read this chapter, what are you trying to tell me, Lord? Do I have areas of judgment or spiritual condescension I have ignored? (List areas He reveals in confession to God.)

  _____
  _____
  _____
  _____

- Father, who are the groups or types of people I am most prone to judge? (List those too.)

  _____
  _____
  _____
  _____

- Who have I offended, Lord, with my judgment? What would You have me do to make this right?

- Lord, help me understand the real need inside me that causes me to appear better, smarter, and more godly than someone else.

- Lord, cleanse this wound that drives me to think and behave like this.

- Now Lord, I have sensed the judging eyes and tongues of people who have hurt me. Please heal my pain and give me Your power to forgive. (List people you forgive.)

_____

_____

_____

_____

- Help me bless each person, one by one, and release each to You to deal with when and how You determine.

Now spend the last few minutes thanking the Lord for the incredible worth and value He placed on you with His fathomless love.

# LEGALISM

## CHAPTER NINETEEN: *David Loveless*

Rules are everywhere. Rules exist for walking across the street, walking our dogs in public, traveling on planes and for strapping babies into carts at the grocery store. In my neighborhood there are rules for house painting, landscaping, even for the type of vehicle parked in a driveway. Some say rules protect good people from bad guys. But rules are useless unless someone good looks after them, administers them, and keeps them right, which is something I discovered one day at my local post office. I kid you not. This is a true story.

Picture your basic government-issue post office with the snake-like stanchions weaving through the room. With no one but me and one man already at the counter, I march through the maze straight to the front. I read a sign on the wall that says:

PLEASE WAIT BEHIND THE WHITE LINE UNTIL YOU ARE CALLED

I glance down to see that my left foot is actually in front of the white line. When the man in front of me completes his transaction, I step to the available clerk and lay down my letter notice. Now the clerk, hands folded on the counter, doing nothing, looks me square in the eye and says, "Sir, I'm sorry. You need to go back behind the white line." I am confused. I ask why. She says, "Because I didn't call you yet." I say, "But the man you were helping is gone and I am next." She says, "I'm sorry sir, but didn't you read the sign? You are not supposed to step across the white line until you are called."

You've got to be kidding me. I muster all of the fruits of the Spirit I can but certain ones do not respond. Then she says, "If you want me to help you, you need to go back behind the white line." Incredulous, I comply. She waits a few moments then announces, to no one but me—the only person in the room, "May I help the next person in line?"

Some rules are good (like the ones made to protect innocent postal workers from unruly crowds). But man-contrived, religious rules can suck all the God-life out of good, innocent believers.

Like this woman from our survey: "[Leaders] constantly scrutinized the number of people we invited to church or the spiritual level of our prayers. At one meeting, they actually read a published list of people's sins. Keeping the requirements correctly and being baptized might be enough to admit you to Heaven. They intentionally held people in fear by demanding attendance at every meeting and recreational function, and issuing approval of housemates and work places." When she finally denounced this ridged, unhealthy behavior this woman said, "I was ostracized. I lost friends, my whole church family. It was devastating. I have known people to breakdown over this kind of thing."

Tragically, this brand of religiosity is not a rare report in the Kingdom of God.

## THE FIDDLER ON YOUR ROOF

Spiritual legalism elevates the religious inventions of man above the atoning grace of Jesus. It designs principles that adhere to *tradition* rather than seeking the true spirit behind the statues of God. Legalism emphasizes obedience to regulations or conforming to prescribed behavior which, even for the most enthusiastic believer, can never be perfectly executed.

*"One Sabbath, Jesus was strolling with His disciples through a field of ripe grain. Hungry, the disciples were pulling off the heads of grain and munching on them. Some Pharisees reported them to Jesus: 'Your disciples are breaking the Sabbath rules!' Jesus said, 'Really? Didn't you ever read what David and his companions did when they were hungry, how they entered the sanctuary and ate fresh bread off the altar, bread that no one but priests were allowed to eat? And didn't you ever read in God's Law that priests carrying out their Temple duties break Sabbath rules all the time and it's not held against them? There is far more at stake here than religion. If you had any idea what this Scripture meant—'I prefer a flexible heart to an inflexible ritual'—you wouldn't be nitpicking like this. The Son of Man is no lackey to the Sabbath; He's in charge.'*

*"When Jesus left the field, He entered their meeting place. There was a man there with a crippled hand. They said to Jesus, 'Is it legal to heal on the Sabbath?' They were baiting Him. He replied, 'Is there a person here who, finding one of your lambs fallen into a ravine, wouldn't, even though it was a Sabbath, pull it out? Surely kindness to people is as legal as kindness to animals!' Then He said to the man, 'Hold out your hand.' He held it out and it was healed. The Pharisees walked out furious, sputtering about how they were going to ruin Jesus." (Matthew 12:1–14, The Message)*

The Pharisees were great rule keepers. In this case, the Pharisees established (or embellished) multiple rules that added to God's commandment to remember the Sabbath and keep it holy. They believed they served God and the people's best interest by defining God's commandment: rest on the Sabbath.

Jesus was after relationship. Many times, Jesus intentionally violated Hebrew laws. To get a reaction? Maybe. To create a platform for dialogue? Probably. He emphasized holiness found in a love relationship with God. Certainly God hates sin and is crushed by willful rejection of Him. But Jesus exposed fakers, actors, showmen, and perfectionists because He knew their form of religion blocked everyone from embracing His grace.

Where Jesus' discipleship was approachable, humble, and compassionate, others were rigid, relentless and heartless.

### YOU'RE IN THE ARMY NOW

Early in my spiritual journey, I read a book about a man who founded one of the most influential Christian organizations of the 20th century. Along with the stories of people he helped, the book outlined an intense system of discipleship. In part of his plan the men:

- Read their Bible every single day. If, upon going to bed at night, remembered that they had not fulfilled this duty, they should rise and read a portion of scripture before going to sleep.

- Share the gospel with at least one person everyday. If, upon going to bed at night, remembered they had not yet complied, they should rise and look for someone to share with before going back to bed!

The book also narrated times this man became angry if his disciples failed to strictly adhere to his rules for following Christ.

Still, I admired his deep heart for God, his passionate pursuit to disciple, and his influence as a leader. I did not immediately see the error in his rigorous regime. I followed his prescribed pattern and it just about killed me. I discovered my heart shrinking toward God and others. So intent on performing the right activities and finishing my checklists, I hardly noticed the fading love and grace of God.

We know danger lurks when the duties of discipleship douse our desire for relationship.

The Apostle Paul, who earlier in his life had been the consummate rule keeper, lets people in on a revelation that set him free.

> *"So don't put up with anyone pressuring you in details of diet, worship services, or holy days. All those things are mere shadows cast before what was to come; the substance is Christ.*

> *"Don't tolerate people who try to run your life, ordering you to bow and scrape, insisting that you join their obsession... They're completely out of touch with the source of life, Christ, who puts us together in one piece, whose very breath and blood flow through us. He is the Head and we are the body. We can grow up healthy in God only as He nourishes us.*

*"So, then, if with Christ you've put all that pretentious and infantile religion behind you, why do you let yourselves be bullied by it? 'Don't touch this! Don't taste that! Don't go near this!' Do you think things that are here today and gone tomorrow are worth that kind of attention? Such things sound impressive if said in a deep enough voice. They even give the illusion of being pious and humble and ascetic. But they're just another way of showing off, making yourselves look important."*
*(Colossians 2:16–23, The Message)*

## AN INSIDE JOB

Legalism overemphasizes some form of outward participation and neglects inward transformation. But before you think I am glossing over the importance of doing good, consider what comes first. Jesus' emphasis focused first on inner change that then fuels outward behavior. Remember, He chastised the Pharisees for cleaning only the "outside of the cup" and encouraged them to "first wash the inside."

Surrounded by zealous legalism within the early church, Paul wrote an entire letter about it to the Galatians. Paul called legalism a different gospel. He reminded everyone that God gave His laws to convince us of our perpetual imperfection and that, unless a sinless Savior intervened, we would be condemned to eternal separation from Him.

Still, something in many Christians demands that everyone, especially the brethren, should maintain the perception of perfection.

## FRIDAY NIGHT BLIGHT

One Friday night, some years ago, our son was playing in a football game for his Christian high school. At one point the referee threw a penalty flag and called a foul on our son. In the heat of the moment he reacted angrily and yelled at the referee. Suddenly, the school principal ran onto the field, grabbed our son and shouted, "Young man, a real Christian does not act like that! How can you call yourself a Christian?"

Now I wish my son had responded better. Certainly the ref was right to throw the flag. But the principal's reaction could not have been more wrong-headed. What my son, all the guys on his team, and anyone else within ear-shot actually heard was that true Christ-followers never, ever, ever mess up.

### YOU *MIGHT* BE A LEGALIST IF...

If you are still not sure if some of your beliefs or practices are rooted in legalism let me put it in a way that might be easier to understand.

You might be a legalist if...

- You sport ten Christian bumper stickers on your car, two of which boldly declare the official date of the Second Coming of Jesus.

- You wear noise-canceling headphones in the mall to avoid hearing non-Christian music.

- You do not own a television or computer and believe it is wrong to attend anything but a "G" (or in special cases "PG") rated movie.

- You believe those who wear certain clothes, or get tattoos or body piercings are evil and judge them either openly or in your heart.

- You have issues with people who smoke, drink in moderation, or dance even the Virginia Reel.

- You believe your Bible translation is the only one with God's Good Christian Seal of Approval.

- You believe your way to do church is the best and spurn the way other Christians, especially the ones on certain cable channels, express their faith.

- You believe God is miffed if you fail or forget to read His Word or pray each day with your eyes closed for at least 30 minutes at 5am —on your knees.

- You believe God is angry with you when you sin.

- You believe you are not a good Christian when you miss church or Bible study and/or lift an eyebrow when others don't show up.

- You believe all Christians should belong to the same political party and support the same candidate.

## RELEASE FROM THE TRAP OF LEGALISM

Legalism is a trap that we can be deeply caught in. If you realize your need to be un-stuck here are some practical steps:

*1. Realize that TRUSTING not TRYING is what got you into a right relationship with God, and is what keeps you there.*

Meditate on this passage:

"Now God has us where he wants us, with all the time in this world and the next to shower grace and kindness upon us in Christ Jesus. Saving is all his idea, and all his work. All we do is trust him enough to let him do it. It's God's gift from start to finish! We don't play the major role. If we did, we'd probably go around bragging that we'd done the whole thing! No, we neither make nor save ourselves. God does both the making and saving." (Ephesians 2:7–9, The Message)

*2. Release people with different Christian convictions than yours.*

If they are wrong, God can handle them. Do not waste your time or presume the duty of measuring levels of faith. Take your cues from this scripture:

"For instance, a person who has been around for a while might well be convinced that he can eat anything on the table, while another, with a different background, might assume he should only be a vegetarian and eat accordingly. But since both are guests at Christ's table, wouldn't it be terribly rude if they fell to criticizing what the other ate or didn't eat? God, after all, invited them both to the table. Do you have any business crossing people off the guest list or interfering with God's welcome? If there are corrections to be made or manners to be learned, God can handle that without your help." (Romans 14:2–4, The Message)

*3. With Jesus' blessing, dismiss legalistic teachers and churches.*

Do not think yourself spiritual enough to show them their error. Though it is painful to uproot long-held relationships, a move to plant yourself in an authentic, grace-based Christ-centered church will bring joy and spiritual freedom you never dreamed possible.

Such is now the experience of the woman mentioned earlier. Today she says, "When others start criticizing the Church or Christians, I try to remind them that it's really about a relationship with Christ not the shortcomings of people. It's finally so refreshing to hear about the love of Christ. My church doesn't let you off the hook though. It explains God's expectations for my life. I'm learning ways to please Him without being a legalist."

# POSSESSIVENESS

## CHAPTER TWENTY: *David Loveless*

At the moment, we have six grandchildren under the age of seven. They call me "G-daddy." I invented this name so that no matter how old I get I will always *sound* hip. I would like to report they are all angelic, 24/7. But apparently they have a slightly fallen nature inherited from some other side of the family. We might be enveloped in a cloud of blissful harmony when someone inevitably bursts out with, "It's mine, G-daddy! Tell her she can't have it!"

Kids do not come with a generous heart. And sometimes, neither do full-grown, God-blessed adults.

### GOING, GOING, GONE

Many years ago, some people in our church decided to leave us and go to a church pastored by a friend of mine across town. Upon further inquiry, I discovered this pastor had met privately with the group, heard their complaints and welcomed them as members. I would *like* to report all nine of the fruits of the Spirit were fully operational in me at this revelation. And I would *like* to say this did not offend me because, after all, we are all part of the same spiritual family. But I would be lying. I was chapped. I tried to be chapped "in the Spirit" but nope. I was flat out chapped.

Forget for the moment where others may have erred in this drama. Someone was stealing my sheep! These were my people for crying out loud! Had I not faithfully loved them, equipped them, and empowered them? Had I not laid my life down for them?

**MY CHURCH**

We have all used the term "my church." Church members as well as church leaders say this all the time. It's an innocent comment, right? We also talk about "my friends," "my work," "my kids," "my life." And how often do we refer to, "my Porsche," "my Harley," "my yacht," "my country club?" There is a reason they call "my" a possessive pronoun! Over time, it's easy for us to focus on our rights and entitlements instead of our responsibilities. Culture places an ever-increasing emphasis on individual rights as opposed to a community committed to the common good.

Just as an experiment, I wonder if a person could omit the word "my" for an entire day?

When we give our lives to Christ as Lord, in essence we offer Him the keys of ownership, complete access and control of all our earthly belongings. In time He brings people and places and projects for us to cultivate for Him for whatever length of time He deems sufficient. The goal is for us to remain in total trust mode. We know Jesus promises to *provide* everything we need: spiritually, emotionally, relationally, financially—everything. When we clutch possessively to people or positions or even platforms of influence it is a sign we do not really trust the Lord's provision or do not believe He has our best in mind. Keeping anyone or anything contained or corralled is rooted in a fear that God is incapable of managing or disinterested in things important to us.

Written to the wealthy, the principle of 1 Timothy 6:17–18 easily applies to us when it comes to "our" possessions. Here the Lord reminds us, "Command those who are rich in this present world not to be arrogant nor put their hope in wealth, which is so uncertain, but to put their hope in God, who richly provides us with everything for our enjoyment." (NIV) And how many times must we quote Philippians 4:19 before we actually live like we believe that God will meet all our needs according to His glorious riches in Christ Jesus?

As we learn to be generous with people, possessions, positions and places in our lives, it helps to remember that God does not ask anything of us He has not first required of and demonstrated Himself. He could have hoarded His one and only Son but instead He lavishly, sacrificially splurged Him upon the world. In turn, that Savior/Son surrendered His proximity to His Father and His possession of Heavenly splendor in order that we may be eternally rich.

## OWNERSHIP HAS ITS PRIVILEGES

Maybe it would serve us well to once again rehearse exactly to whom the gathered elect lawfully belong.

> *"It was He who gave some to be apostles, some to be prophets, some to be evangelists, and some to be pastors and teachers, to prepare God's people for works of service, so that the body of Christ may be built up." (Ephesians 4:11–12, NIV)*

> *"And I tell you that you are Peter, and on this rock I will build My church, and the gates of Hades will not overcome it." (Matthew 16:18, NIV)*

> *"I am the good shepherd; I know My sheep and My sheep know Me—just as the Father knows Me and I know the Father—and I lay down My life for the sheep. I have other sheep that are not of this sheep pen. I must bring them also. They too will listen to My voice, and there shall be one flock and one shepherd." (John 10:14–16, NIV)*

Early in my pastoral life, I really wrestled with possessiveness. My wife and I and five couples had planted a church in Vancouver, British Columbia. After being there four years watching God raise a strong, vibrant ministry, to our surprise, He called us to Orlando. Though it did not make human sense to us, we received multiple confirmations to move. But because we started the church we could not let it go. It was our baby. The people felt like our children.

When their new pastor arrived and began axing ministries I had put in place I was stunned. What was wrong with the church before? How could God allow someone to mess up the church we had sacrificed so much to build? Then I learned many of the people we helped lead to Christ, even some leaders, were leaving for other churches in the city. I was beside myself. Was all our hard work wasted?

What I could not see then, I now suspect was God's intentional plan to scatter healthy believers to other churches across the Lower Mainland. To this day, many of these dear friends still stand strong and faithful to the Lord in their local churches. No, these guys were not mine. Their Father had bigger and better plans than my puny mind could comprehend.

It is understandable that possessiveness sometimes happens when people have labored long to help their church gain critical momentum. In a small church it can seem like a near death experience to hear one or more say they no longer need you, they have found someone new. Believe me, I know the feeling.

I have mentioned Caron and I have three sons. I think that THE most difficult parenting point is the day we wake up to realize our children really do not belong to us. Intellectually, we may know they are God's but it is tough to let go having cherished children, bonded with them, protected them, financed them, cheered them, disciplined them and have been responsible for them. We subtly and then fiercely grow an attachment that refuses to break when the time comes. Nevertheless, God intends for us to learn that they are of us but not ours. The tension can complicate and confuse navigation through this season. I think church people and leaders go through many of the same natural heart struggles with their spiritual kids and siblings.

**FREEDOM FROM POSSESSIVENESS**

If someone decides to leave the church where you fellowship, see if there is an unheard voice. If all concerns were spoken and heard and all reconciling possibilities were exhausted then bless the person as he goes with love and prayers. He doesn't belong to your church. He belongs to Jesus. Do not make folks feel guilty for leaving. And do not burn bridges. No matter what, believers are family.

But didn't Paul refer to people he served as his children? How can you shepherd without feeling like you own sheep?

*"As apostles of Christ we could have been a burden to you, but we were gentle among you, like a mother caring for her little children. We loved you so much that we were delighted to share with you not only the gospel of God but our lives as well, because you had become so dear to us... For you know that we dealt with each of you as a father deals with his own children, encouraging, comforting and urging you to live lives worthy of God, who calls you into his kingdom and glory." (1 Thessalonians 2:5–9, 11–12, NIV)*

Notice that Paul says we were 'like a mother' and we were 'like a father' but he never claims himself their literal parent. He cared for them responsibly not possessively.

## ROAMING CHARGES

If you are one who sometimes struggles when your pastor is away for training or ministry, let me say as one who sometimes does this, such times can greatly boost his ministry. Excursions beyond your church walls can infuse a leader with spiritual vitality. He often comes back appreciating his own church even more. Encourage your pastors to participate in appropriate amounts of healthy diversion. Iron does sharpen iron, making a leader more focused, energized and better equipped.

What about when people go church hopping?

Almost every week someone approaches me in the lobby to say he is visiting from another church. We did not invite him. We did not market him. We do not want to cause problems with his church. He shows up for a multitude of reasons. Here is how our staff and I handle these situations.

We tell people we are honored to have them and hope they had a fresh, meaningful encounter with the Lord that day. Then we seek to commend the church they are coming from. A common reference might be: "I am sure First Community Church is a great church that seeks to honor God and serve people just like we do."

I then ask if I can know why they are visiting from across town. I tell them people leave churches for a variety of reasons. Some are legitimate. But some people are running from something.

I ask if there are any unresolved relational issues with the previous church leadership or anyone who attends there. If they respond affirmatively, I encourage them to seek to resolve them.

If they tell me they did not agree with the direction or doctrine of their church I ask them if, at any time, they expressed their concerns. If they tell me they did not I encourage them to go back and do so.

## WITH HEARTS AND HANDS WIDE OPEN

While writing this chapter, an interesting experiment took place in our city. Joel Hunter is a friend of mine who pastors one of the largest churches in America, Northland Community Church. Though Northland is nearly twice our size we both pastor well-respected churches in our area. Over the years people have left one church to attend the other's church. But to demonstrate we really believe there is actually only one church in Orlando we decided to try what many would call a bold move. We decided to swap churches for a weekend.

The response from both congregations was electric. Attendees loved hearing from someone new and were ecstatic over the flow of generosity. From my perspective it felt over-the-top-cool to wholeheartedly love, bless and promote the ministry of a sister church just up the road.

Did I have any fear that one of the best teachers and pastors in America would end up stealing sheep from our flock? Truthfully, no. Clearly, I am aware some at our church might prefer Joel's preaching to mine. But at this point in my life, I can say I am good with that because I believe none of the folks at Discovery Church belong to me!

John the Baptist mentors me in this understanding. There is so much about his life and character I admire. He calls it like he sees it and never doubts his assignment. John's disciples come to him and say, "Rabbi, that man who was with you on the other side of the Jordan, the one you testified about, well, he is baptizing, and everyone is going to him." To this John replied, "A man can receive only what is given him from heaven… the bride belongs to the bridegroom." (John 3: 26–29 NIV)

Arriving at this freedom has not been easy. The realization that everything and everyone ultimately belongs to God comes after much heartache, prayer, revelation and a fair amount of getting it wrong. I have pastored long enough to know I will be tested on this again and again. And even if I do decide to keep my toys in a tight grip, if Jesus needs them, He will pry them loose. All the toys are His. I am learning the grace and joy in being a faithful but temporary manager of the gifts, opportunities, and people God entrusts to my care.

I pray this for you as well.

# ABUSE OF AUTHORITY

## CHAPTER TWENTY ONE: *Francis Anfuso*

*"You can bend it and twist it…You can misuse and abuse it…
But even God cannot change the Truth."*—Michael Levy, British Politician

I grew up in New York City in a very dangerous and violent age. One night, during my freshman year of college, some of my friends and I decided to do something crazy. On a fluke, we drove an hour or so to Coney Island to get Nathan's famous hot dogs. We arrived around three in the morning, purchased the hotdogs, and were about to leave.

Suddenly, fifty feet away, a man obviously gifted in martial arts, began to mercilessly beat someone who seemed drunk. Within seconds his helpless victim fell, knocked senseless. I thought he was going to kill him and will never forget the sight of this defenseless man, his passive hands down, being repeatedly hit in the head. It makes me sick to think about it, even decades later. Not looking for a fight we couldn't win, we squirmed our way back into our car, horrified by what we had witnessed.

Violent, physical abuse upon the powerless is one of the most despicable crimes against humanity. Only a monstrous, cold-blooded beast takes advantage of one incapable of defense.

It makes us mad, enraged really, when an adult molests a child, a leader intimidates a follower, or worse yet, someone representing God preys upon one he should protect.

Irish Statesman Edmund Burke once wrote, "The greater the power, the more dangerous the abuse." Here we see a key ingredient in any abusive encounter: the powerful takes advantage of the powerless—a tyrant victimizes the vulnerable.

## DEFINING ABUSE

In a free culture or church environment, priceless liberties abound. We have freedom of speech and response. We are free to love—even hate. But, when liberty becomes a license for lawlessness it results in abuse. President James Madison wrote, "Liberty may be endangered by the abuse of liberty, but also by the abuse of power."

Abuse can be defined three ways:

1.  to speak in an insulting and offensive way to or about

2.  to use or treat in such a way as to cause damage or harm

3.  to treat with cruelty or violence, regularly or repeatedly

As we can see, many faces of abuse produce pain that spans a spectrum ranging from discouragement to outright trauma. I have personally experienced the first two levels of abuse in church, and all three of them in my childhood home. The very nature of abuse evokes an avalanche of unwanted memories.

Some of you reading this chapter have turned to it first because the third, crueler level of abuse is your own experience. Hardly a week goes by without my hearing another tragic story of abuse from some battered soul. In the *Church Wounds Survey*, so many abusive situations were recounted that I just cried upon reading them.

*Abuse of authority* is one of the more common church wounds. 31% of all respondents confessed to it. Only *judgmentalism, leader insensitivities,* and *hypocrisy* were more prevalent in our survey. According to descriptions of abuse provided, the most widespread violation surrounded *leaders using guilt and shame to manipulate others.* As a control mechanism, at times abuse involved sex. More commonly a self-obsessed leader applied abuse to retain power. Pockets of cruelty on our planet are not surprising, but when church leaders use their position and authority to dominate and violate, a torrent of rage rises within us. These abuses demand justice. Judgment must be executed.

Yet, responses to abuse swell with potential danger.

## REMEDY OR RETALIATION

Many times in life, the quick fix is the wrong remedy. The Bible repeatedly stresses this from a variety of angles. No matter what has happened to us or those we love, it is less than helpful if our response is retaliatory. Matters become worse when we attempt to overcome evil with evil. Consider these priceless admonitions. "Do not be overcome by evil, but overcome evil with good." (Romans 12:21, NKJV)

Jesus further challenged, "But I say to you, love your enemies, bless those who curse you, do good to those who hate you, and pray for those who spitefully use you." (Matthew 5:44, NKJV) And, "But I say, don't resist an evil person! If you are slapped on the right cheek, turn the other, too." (Matthew 5:39) Also, "Do not give to the foolish man a foolish answer, or you will be like him." (Proverbs 26:4, BBE)

We were not created to be the dispensers of God's wrath. "For we know the One who said, 'Vengeance is mine, I will repay,' and again, 'The Lord will judge His people.'" (Hebrews 10:30, NET)

It will take great trust to place our own injustice in the hands of the only Person who can balance the scales. If we veer from the path of life outlined by God's Word, we will merely bring down the judgment we hoped for others upon ourselves.

In the following section, as we review accounts of abuse within the church, and consider an appropriate response, may we see with God's eyes, and feel with His heart. "Human anger does not accomplish God's righteousness." (James 1:20, NET)

## THE PAIN OF ABUSE

Comments from people who were abused by Christian leaders are many and varied. Here is a small sampling of direct quotes from our *Church Wounds Survey.*

> *"Our family was devastated by the response of leadership to abuses (sexual and otherwise) that occurred."*

*"When I came out of it, I had a hard time trying to figure out what was God and what was human abuse."*

*"I helped start a church with a narcissist who misused his prophetic gifting to manipulate the men and women in the church to be dependent on him instead of Christ for their healing. He also lied to many of the women in the church and manipulated them into submitting to him sexually 'as part of their healing.'"*

*"I think the abuse of authority was most hurtful to me. When we tried to leave a particular church we were told by the pastor, his wife and the leadership that we were deceived and not in God's will."*

*"Our church wounds were a result of the shepherding movement. We were part of that type of church for nine very painful years. Legalism robs a person of the joy that naturally is part of the redeemed life."*

*"Being 'in covenant' with the church meant you couldn't leave the church without permission or being 'released to go.' I still have a great deal of anger at the seemingly 'injustice' of it all. I think (I hope) I've moved out of the hate. Of the many families who left the church shortly after we did, probably 80% or more have either divorced, separated or have teens who have left the house."*

Though absolutely wretched, God can redeem and bring value to any abusive situation. Here are some of the courageous responses of those who intentionally refused to let abuse define them.

*"The season of spiritual abuse was the most intensely deep time with the Lord that I have ever had in my life. I experienced the very deep things of God for the first time in my life, but, at the same time, was experiencing deep spiritual abuse. I would not be the person I am in the Lord today if it were not for this experience so I wouldn't trade it even though it was terrible."*

*"My pastor used guilt to manipulate people to do what he wanted them to do for the church. When you felt burnt out from serving too long, it was really hard to leave because you were made to feel guilty for leaving the church. Pastors are just people with issues and past hurts like we are, in need of healing themselves like we do. We have to extend grace and mercy and forgiveness, just as we have received these. But staying in that environment is not necessary or healthy, and does not mean we haven't forgiven."*

*"I cannot in one sentence describe the over twenty years of deceit, lying, and greed that I later found was true about the pastor I served with all of my heart for most all of those years. I thought I was serving a man of God. He was actually a self-serving, lying, greedy, narcissistic abuser... I call myself a recovering Christian. I have never stopped going to church because I know God, my Father, desires it. I know that He loves me and He is proving it to me almost daily, restoring my faith, and showing me that He understands what I've been through. I just wish I had seen the truth about this man years ago. I have a hard time with that part and the harm it did to my family and my marriage. We are still being healed."*

*"Child sexual abuse was covered by the pastor (I am a social worker and previous CPS investigator). I continued going to the Lord with every thought and hurt I would feel. I would journal it and talk to Him about my anger, hurt, not understanding. I also practiced not mulling it over in my mind—I would wrestle the thought captive to Christ. I am not willing to give up my soft heart or new spirit for anything, even if all worldly rational says I have that right, I have no rights but the rightness of Jesus. Ezekiel 36:26, 'And I will give you a new heart with new and right desires, and I will put a new spirit in you. I will take out your stony heart of sin and give you a new, obedient heart.'"*

## MYSTIFYING ACCOUNTS

As you read these comments, recognize that all descriptions are one-sided. No spouse, leader, or pastor was able to contradict or balance the accusations mentioned here. That being said, here are some mystifying accounts extracted from the survey.

*"When seeking pastoral counseling after being physically abused by my husband, the pastor told me if I were a better wife, he wouldn't have to treat me this way... God has shown me the power of forgiveness, without which healing cannot begin. He has taught me it's okay to reach out to those who believe differently as they are still my brothers and sisters. Their prayers are just as valid as mine. He has also revealed to me the importance of knowing the difference between 'thus saith the Lord' and 'thus saith the church.'"*

*"My husband shared with our pastor something private about his life assuming the pastor's confidentiality. The pastor told everybody he was close with in the church, including youth, not to help anybody but just to gossip... God revealed to me that it was a blessing in disguise. I grew so much closer to God through this situation. I*

*stop depending on people to bring me closer and started depending on God alone."*

When another woman described what hurt most about her church wounds, she replied, "My children, being so wounded in the church, don't desire to do church even though they were brought up in it. Leaving the church helped me break the abuse. There was then a lot of prayer to release bitterness and anger. But real healing came when I attended a healthy church and was loved on and appreciated by leaders. It was sunshine after years of dark clouds that totally freed me to have joy again."

She continued her response with great insight. "Very few churches have been transparent and dealt with the fact that we are those same people, wounds and all, who come into the church. Our wounds were not all healed when we accepted Christ. People assume the leadership of the church have had healing or are getting healed so they can be an example of spiritual health. My own woundings, not necessarily church wounds, play a large role in my focus and how I respond to church wounds. The healthier I am, the more effective I will be at understanding how to process any wounding. I now ask myself, 'What is the Lord wanting to change in me?' Because it's never just about the person who wounded us."

Who can better share with us about the healing process than someone who has been healed?

One wise woman shared, "God will not fail us; people will. We need to anchor in Him, not in other people. Pastors are to serve, not to be elevated to a special status. When we see wrongdoing, in love, we need to pursue help. After the Lord completely healed me from all I had been through, (there was abuse in the home as well), I was given the opportunity to help others by leading a support group for wounded women for about 3–4 years. 'Though you have made me see troubles, many and bitter, you will restore my life again; from the depths of the earth you will again bring me up. You will increase my honor and comfort me once again.'" (Psalm 71:20, 21, NIV)

Let me end this chapter with a summary perspective. The healing process in our emotions and heart will not be instantaneous. But, little by little, each forgiving step along the way—each humbling acknowledgement—each broken confession—and each prayerful entreaty before God will, without a doubt, bring us closer and closer to the miraculous healing Jesus promised.

God's Word offers resounding encouragement: "So don't get tired of doing what is good. Don't get discouraged and give up, for we will reap a harvest of blessing at the appropriate time." (Galatians 6:9)

# ELITISM

Section Six

# SELF-CENTEREDNESS

## CHAPTER TWENTY TWO: *Francis Anfuso*

*"Egotists are always me-deep in conversation."*—Anonymous

The greatest enemy to our being as free as God intended is not sin, but self!

The self-centeredness of others may have caused hurt, but obsession with self perpetuates it.

Jesus already took care of our sins when He died on the Cross. Now we must die to self in order to be truly free. Freedom is ahead, when self is behind! This is the real battleground for church wounds.

Self is always the culprit at the epicenter of each wound found in every chapter of this book: dashed expectations, misunderstandings, offenses, promises unfulfilled, hypocrisy, misrepresentation, half-truths, financial impropriety, immorality, inappropriate behavior, leader insensitivities, believer insensitivities, misuse of gifts of the spirit, pride, spiritual condescension, judgmentalism, legalism, possessiveness, abuse of authority, favoritism, cliques, elitism, church politics, doctrinal divisions, and church splits.

In short, all church wounds have their roots in a preoccupation with self.

As I examined hundreds of the church wounds on our survey, I saw four primary responses: *hostility, hurt, hindrance* and *healing*. Our reaction to church wounds will fit into one or more of these categories. Many feel *hostility* to God and His people because they are more attached to self than the Savior. Past *hurts* fester, becoming far more than a *hindrance*, unless we hunger for the *healing* only Jesus can give.

## HOSTILE RESPONSE

Those who remain *hostile* due to a wounding in life have removed themselves from the healing process. This is tragic! Wounds decay in an endless
loop of anger and self-pity. Breaking this cycle of poor response will
propel us into a lengthy, yet purposeful, journey of forgiveness. If we
seek to understand with humble, yielded hearts, we will eventually be
healed. If we refuse to budge, rehashing the hurt inflicted by others,
then the pain grows deeper. At times our present condition indicates
our commitment: stewing or healing, remembering or reconciling.

Paul wrote, "For there is a root of sinful self-interest in us that is at odds
with a free spirit, just as the free spirit is incompatible with selfishness."
(Galatians 5:17a, The Message)

Only God is the judge of thoughts and intentions, but Christians, especially
leaders, must realize that selfish inconsistencies and hypocrisies stumble
others. One *Church Wounds Survey* respondent wrote, "The pastor and his
wife each showed up in new cars only weeks after asking, (and receiving),
huge 'sacrificial' giving. And there were many financially hurting people in
the congregation."

The intensity of hostility toward those who have hurt us often parallels
the severity of wounding. Consequently, we need time to bounce back
from wounds. But, more than time, we need God-given wisdom and
understanding.

Consider this. What percentage of your emotional hole, did the person who
hurt you dig? And what portion have you dug, and are continuing to dig?

Jesus challenged us to stop digging when He said: "Do not judge others,
and you will not be judged. For you will be treated as you treat others. The
standard you use in judging is the standard by which you will be judged.
And why worry about a speck in your friend's eye when you have a log in
your own? How can you think of saying to your friend, 'Let me help you
get rid of that speck in your eye,' when you can't see past the log in your
own eye? Hypocrite! First get rid of the log in your own eye; then you will
see well enough to deal with the speck in your friend's eye."
(Matthew 7:1–5)

Beyond being mere bystanders on a healing pilgrimage, we are called to follow the One who has suffered most.

> *"For God made Christ, who never sinned, to be the offering for our sin, so that we could be made right with God through Christ." (2Corinthians 5:21)*

> *"But it was our sins that did that to Him, that ripped and tore and crushed Him— our sins! He took the punishment, and that made us whole. Through His bruises we get healed." (Isaiah 53:5, The Message)*

## HURT RESPONSE

*Hurt* individuals always have a choice. Either we seek healing, or wallow in the pain of past offenses. No one escapes the planet *unhurt*. It is the price of admission to the human race: a marathon not for the faint or faultfinding, but for the faithful few who are more humbled by their own shortcomings than the faults of others. Be a pathfinder, not a faultfinder!

The more severe the wounding, the longer the recovery time. But, at some point, I will have to decide: am I on a journey to help others recover, or am I destined to remain a patient? The only person who can make that decision is me.

An incessant review of past wounds inflicted by selfish people yields only a shallow sense of satisfaction. I have merely replaced the self-focus of others for my own. I may be hurt, but am I more committed to being healed, or to reminisce my pain?

The Internet is filled with the commentary of wounded hearts who seem more attached to regurgitating their bitter perspective, angry response, and pointless pain, than fighting to understand, forgive, and be healed. The former chase their offended tail. The latter elevate the significance of circumstance to a redemptive place. Every pain can be exchanged for peace if we allow God to have His way.

> *"Look at that man, bloated by self-importance—full of himself but soul-empty. But the person in right standing before God through loyal and steady believing is fully alive, really alive." (Habakkuk 2:4, The Message)*

I want to be fully alive—full of God. I've had enough of myself!

> *"Then He (Jesus) told them this story: 'The farm of a certain rich man produced a terrific crop. He talked to himself: "What can I do? My barn isn't big enough for this harvest." Then he said, "Here's what I'll do: I'll tear down my barns and build bigger ones. Then I'll gather in all my grain and goods, and I'll say to myself, Self, you've done well! You've got it made and can now retire. Take it easy and have the time of your life!" Just then God showed up and said, "Fool! Tonight you die. And your barn full of goods—who gets it?" That's what happens when you fill your barn with Self and not with God.'" (Luke 12:16–21, The Message)*

What's in your barn, more self or more Savior?

### HINDERED RESPONSE

If we can get past *hostile* and *hurt*, our being *hindered* is not a deal-breaker. Hindrances need not stumble long-term. Woundings are opportunities to be humbled, thereby activating the grace and power of God. (James 4:6) Emotional hindrances do not bind or limit. With an upright heart, past hurts will just drive us closer to God—a divinely ordained focus that, in the end, is always worth it.

Perhaps church wounds are the Mt. Everest of all relational struggles. Those who conquer lesser interpersonal conflicts fare better than those who don't. Yet, all battles in this area reap a comparable reward. The God of love tries us best in relationships that are tested. The metal of character proves itself by allowing God's love to cover even those who hurt us most.

After many days of pouring over the *Church Wound Survey*, I came across a profound comment from someone who certainly had his share of church wounds, but arrived at a refreshing conclusion: "In my time around church, I've been treated with love and respect far more than I've been offended." Bravo! This person did not dwell on the painful offenses; he chose to re-member countless experiences where love and respect were shown. Though I realize some church experiences were devoid of such love and respect, I have known too many people who have intentionally chosen to camp at the offense rather than remember the many good times of which they were privileged to be part.

Herein lies the healthy key for processing all relationships. What we choose to remember will become what we are unable to forget. If I choose to remember God's forgiveness toward my own selfishness, then I will be less preoccupied with the self-fixation of others.

> *"Obsession with self in these matters is a dead end; attention to God leads us out into the open, into a spacious, free life. Focusing on the self is the opposite of focusing on God. Anyone completely absorbed in self ignores God, ends up thinking more about self than God. That person ignores who God is and what He is doing."* *(Romans 8:6–7, The Message)*

When Jesus shared what is now known as the *Golden Rule*, "Do for others as you would like them to do for you," (Luke 6:31) He wasn't hoping that we would wish others were less selfish toward us. He intended that we would rise above the selfish misbehavior of others, and model, by our own actions, kind and sensitive treatment. The *Golden Rule* was designed to change *our* behavior, not to make it the standard by which we grade others.

Jesus said, "Do to others," not, "Expect others to do for you."

> *"Love never gives up. Love cares more for others than for self. Love doesn't want what it doesn't have. Love doesn't strut, doesn't have a swelled head."* *(1 Corinthians 13:4, The Message)*

### HEALED RESPONSE

Being *healed* from past hurts will depend upon processing *offense*. *Healing* is the goal, but *offense* is the *hurdle*. Understand that some wounds come from our own insecurities and therefore make us more susceptible to certain wounding. (Jeremiah 17:9, Ephesians 4:32) Yet, be persuaded that there is redemptive value in every situation in life. (Romans 8:28)

Falling prey to the mistakes and improprieties of others is not uncommon. (John 8:7) The danger of focusing on selfishness is that the virus infects us. Self must be quarantined, or it will spread like a cancer. The Message paraphrase provides a unique perspective in these words of Jesus, "Self-help is no help at all. Self-sacrifice is the way, My way, to finding yourself, your true self." (Matthew 16:25)

Someone willing to be healed will recognize these truths. A proper response to pain births a passion to help others. Loving counsel does not blame or "pile on." We must earnestly desire every leader to minister life to God's people and every wounded soul to experience healing. (Ephesians 4:11–17, 1Chronicles 16:22, Romans 13:7)

Attitudes reveal motive. If the intention is restoration, then words become healing balm. If the goal is retaliation, then safety is at risk. Like suicide bombers, revenge will explode—only to maim the innocent. Jesus said, "You can't keep your true self hidden forever; before long you'll be exposed. You can't hide behind a religious mask forever; sooner or later the mask will slip and your true face will be known." (Luke 12:2, The Message)

The most selfish person I've ever known is me.

I've not only seen the fault of my actions in the pain of others, I've had a ringside seat to my heart and unearthed the motive behind the madness. The only way I can become less incensed by others' selfishness, is to examine the full consequence of my own words and deeds.

I can only offer the mercy I have received. Second-hand mercy is mere counterfeit. "For there will be no mercy for you if you have not been merciful to others. But if you have been merciful, then God's mercy toward you will win out over His judgment against you." (James 2:13) "The whole point of what we're urging is simply love—love uncontaminated by self-interest and counterfeit faith, a life open to God." (1Timothy 1:5, The Message)

We know we are healed when we pray with every ounce of passion for those who have hurt us. We know we have the Healer's heart when we petition God to bind their wounds even before He tends to ours. This will require perhaps the greatest miracle of all. Only then will we make God's "joy complete by being like-minded, having the same love, being one in spirit and purpose." (Philippians 2:2, NIV)

Become like Jesus by embracing the privilege to "not be overcome by evil, but overcome evil with good." (Romans 12:21, NKJV)

May we rise to overcome!

# FAVORITISM

## CHAPTER TWENTY THREE: *Francis Anfuso*

I've had lots of favorites: favorite teams, foods, friends, places, movies, books, scriptures, and a multitude of favorite memories. Even as I type these words, the fresh scent of multiplied favorites refreshes my soul. With the freedom of choice, God grants the joy of personal preference.

Blue is my favorite color.

My wife is my favorite person.

The Bible is my favorite book.

Over and over again, favorites fill the world with color, removing the grey blandness from our lives. People, places and things are truly special.

Though much of favoritism in life is healthy, there are times when a biased, partisan view is not just limiting, but unhealthy. A favorite race can lead to racism. A preference of one child over another can produce a life-long estrangement.

When Peter the Jewish Apostle realized that God's intent was to engraft Gentiles (non-Jews) into His giant family, he wrote, "I now truly understand that God does not show favoritism in dealing with people." (Acts 10:34, NET) In this case, lack of favoritism opened up a world opportunities. God loves everyone equally; He gave us each a special part Himself.

## THE COMPARISON GAME

Having been both a twin and the father of identical twin daughters, Deborah and Havilah, I have experienced first-hand the blessing of intentional equality and the pain of inappropriate preference.

In my childhood, the comparison between my twin brother Joseph and I was not helpful to either of us. He was shorter but earned better grades. I was taller but felt like I wasn't the sharpest tack in the box. We were reminded of both incessantly. It placed an unnecessary strain upon our relationship for many years. Thankfully that has been healed, but not before we both suffered competitiveness that divided our mutual appreciation for one another.

Having grown up acutely aware of sibling preference, I purposed to provide my daughters with a healthier perspective. As they were old enough to understand, I shared that they were *each my favorite,* describing the myriad of marvelous qualities I could see in both of them.

As a young family, Suzie and I spent long car rides pointing out the wonderful qualities we saw in one another, and one area we believed, if changed, would help the other person. All of us were affirmed by the astute observations and challenged to change by encouragements spoken in a loving atmosphere.

Though the inevitable comparison between my identical twin daughters surfaces on a regular basis, a foundation of affirming their individual uniqueness has kept them the closest of friends even now, married with children. Until recently, they had adjacent homes that shared back yards. Their children are growing up more as siblings than cousins. It is a joy to behold the freedom individual respect and appreciation, without favoritism, can afford.

But such is not the case in many families and churches.

## NASTY NEPOTISM

Nepotism is when people in authority favor relatives or friends, especially by giving them jobs. If you have suffered Church Wounds due to the preferential treatment of others, then the pain of partiality is personal. Twenty-three percent of our *Church Wounds Survey* respondents admit this. They, or others they cared about, were mistreated and overlooked due to inappropriate favoritism. Leadership sacrificed a greater good at the expense of pleasing a family member or close friend.

Over the years I have seen my own children and their spouses come and go from our church staff. Presently one is full-time and another is part-time. I have relied heavily on the Holy Spirit's leading and the wise counsel of other leaders to ensure God's preference in the matter. Decisions related to my family members must remain consistent with the will of God and greater good of our church family.

Ironically, both of my daughters have felt my efforts to be fair and above reproach with them in relationship to their church profile. This effort has, at times, caused them to feel less than valued. We've had more than a few tearful conversations when I needed to reaffirm my heart for them. I believe these agonizing exercises test our love for one another and our commitment to do what is right even though we may not be fully understood.

I've also needed to hear the wise counsel of my exceedingly balanced wife, Suzie, reminding me, "Francis, you are their dad first. Always make them feel lovingly fathered, no matter what the situation, or what the decision." If I had perfectly executed this advice I wouldn't have had to hear it as often as I have.

As James, the brother of Jesus who knew about needless comparison, wrote, "the wisdom that comes from Heaven is... without partiality." (James 3:17, 26) So too, we are called to wisely love without partiality and without bias that makes others feel second rate.

**FAVORITISM FOLLIES**

Some of the greatest relational breaches recorded in the Bible occurred due to favoritism. The Book of Genesis recounts story after story of a parent favoring one child over another so much so that hatred, strife and attempted murder resulted.

In the Book of Genesis, childless Abram and Sarai were so desperate to have a baby that they arranged for their handmaiden, Hagar, to conceive a child whom they named Ishmael. (Genesis 16) But the child was not God's intended heir to Abraham's generational blessing.

Later on when the elderly Sarai (now called Sarah) conceived, their son Isaac became heir to the birthright and blessing, not Ishmael. Abram (now called Abraham) preferred Ishmael and Sarah preferred Isaac. The tension between parents and children over who was most favored became so acute that Hagar and her son, Ishmael, were eventually banished from the entire family. (Genesis 21) The division of this estranged family continues now for thousands of years and is at the epicenter of the entire Arab–Israeli conflict. The Arab/Muslim nations are the descendants of Ishmael, while the Israelites come from the lineage of Abraham, Isaac and Jacob.

You would have thought Abraham and Sarah's son, Isaac, would have learned a life-lesson from the foolish favoritism of his childhood. Yet history will repeat itself unless we break the curse of generations past. When he had his own children, Isaac favored his son, Esau, while his wife, Rebekah, preferred Esau's twin, Jacob. Once again, partiality led to massive deception in which Jacob tricked Esau birthright and blessing. (Genesis 27)

The result: "Esau hated Jacob because he had stolen his blessing, and he said to himself, 'My father will soon be dead and gone. Then I will kill Jacob.'" (Genesis 27:41) Because of this favoritism fiasco, Jacob fled for his life for two decades.

More than a coincidence or habit, the relational bondage continued for generations. Even after Jacob's long exile from his parents, he still repeated the dysfunction. When he himself had children, Jacob preferred the children of his favorite wife, Rachel. Her offspring, Joseph and Benjamin, received special treatment over the ten sons born to different wives and handmaids. Consequently, jealousy and resentment caused Joseph's brothers to sell him into slavery and lie to their father, Jacob.

Devastation after devastation perpetuated thousands of years of inter-family feuding and has kept the Middle East as the powder keg of the planet.

Favoritism is death to healthy relationships.

## PARTIAL PASTORS

If the scourge of favoritism can scar nations and entire people groups, how much more will it ravage in a church environment? The *Church Wounds Survey* did not lack for first-hand accounts of these relational breaches. One woman wrote of being stumbled because "favorites were given positions, gifts, cars and money." Another shared, "Depending on your contribution or talent as a musician you were shown favoritism." Inappropriate partiality did not go unnoticed.

Favoritism in the *Church Wounds Survey* was reported even among members of the pastor's family. "Our pastor's wife had so much fear that she created cliques, calling them intercessors, and they became her favorites. She would listen only to them. Everyone else became a threat. Consequently, these women believed that they were 'higher' than the other women. After awhile the other women were not even allowed to pray for each other. Only the special ones could pray."

It is grievous to consider possible injustices and inequities amongst God's people if leaders do not vigilantly put aside their personal preference and allow the Holy Spirit to choose whom He will. The Message sums it up quite well, "Since this is the kind of life we have chosen, the life of the Spirit, let us make sure that we do not just hold it as an idea in our heads or a sentiment in our hearts, but work out its implications in every detail of our lives." (Galatians 5:25, The Message)

As I traveled for nearly two decades throughout the Body of Christ, I encountered many churches where the positioning of family members in leadership roles seemed more than appropriate and evidenced clear blessing upon a godly family. Because of the faithfulness and integrity of both parents and children, a marvelous family legacy had been created. The Bible says, "The generation of the upright will be blessed." (Psalm 112:2b, NKJV) It is wonderful to behold when favor from Heaven is God-breathed.

On the other hand, there were occasions when a potential legacy had become a dynasty. An unworthy relative or friend assumed a position of influence and leadership without sufficiency. Such blatant bias can undermine all the good that God intended.

Certainly the Old Testament provides many examples of unworthy descendants:

*Patriarchs: Isaac's son, Esau (Genesis 25:27–34, Hebrews 12:16–17)*

*Priests: Moses' brother, Aaron's descendant, Abiathar (1Kings 2:27, 35), Eli's sons (1Samuel 2:12–17)*

*Prophets: Samuel's sons, Joel and Abijah (1Samuel 8:2–5)*

*Kings: David's son, Absalom (2Samuel 15–16), Solomon's son, Rehoboam (1Kings 14:21–31), Hezekiah's son, Manasseh (2Kings 21:1–16), Jotham's son, Ahaz (2Kings 16:2–4)*

The lives of these children of leaders were so out of sync with the heart of God that He withheld His desired generational blessing. In some cases, a godly parent stepped in and accepted the humbling truth that, due to sinful behavior, a son was not worthy to take on the mantle of responsibility. As heartbreaking as this may be, it was far less damaging to the people of God than promoting someone clearly undeserving of leadership.

In other situations, when a parent lacked the integrity and will to prevent a child from elevation to leadership prematurely, God Himself arranged circumstances for the best. God's commitment should be ours as well: He will protect those placed in His care. May we have the courage to do what is right even if those closest to us fail to understand our decision.

"The integrity of the upright guides them, but the unfaithful are destroyed by their duplicity." (Proverbs 11:3, NIV)

My prayer is that Jesus will give each of us the integrity to lead even when it costs us much, the humility to ask forgiveness from those we have hurt, and the tender love to forgive those who have hurt us by the sin of favoritism.

# CLIQUES

*"When he saw the man lying there, he crossed to the other side of the road and passed him by."*—Luke 10:31

When Jesus stood in His hometown synagogue of Nazareth, He proclaimed why the Spirit of the Lord was upon Him. His final impassioned sentence was a call to join God's liberated family. "The Spirit of the LORD is upon Me, because He has anointed Me to preach the gospel to the poor; He has sent Me to heal the brokenhearted, to proclaim liberty to the captives and recovery of sight to the blind, to set at liberty those who are oppressed; to proclaim the acceptable year of the LORD." (Luke 4:18–19, NKJV)

Here was a joyous invitation—a "come one, come all" from the God of love. Come partake of the sweet fellowship Heaven enjoys! The life you always wanted was now on the horizon for all to enjoy. He was sent to heal the broken, to set free the bruised and battered, to offer love without reservation.

This exceptional message was first shared with those who had watched Him grow up. At first, His eloquent appeal was well-received. Folks embraced what He had shared. "All who were there spoke well of Him and were amazed by the gracious words that fell from His lips." (Luke 4:22)

Yet within minutes the tide turned. When Jesus candidly exposed their deep resistance to God's Spirit, they became enraged, "all those in the synagogue, when they heard these things, were filled with wrath, and rose up and thrust Him out of the city; and they led Him to the brow of the hill on which their city was built, that they might throw Him down over the cliff." (Luke 4:28–29, NKJV)

From *hero* to *zero* in 60 seconds!

What should have been exuberant joy for all mankind became misunderstanding and adamant rejection of God's heart. If only this response were an ancient relic of some past disconnect, an astounding aberration that time would clear up.

Unfortunately, it is not.

The God of love is still being misunderstood, every day, in countless ways.

## THE CLAQUE OF CLIQUES

The word clique was at one time considered the equivalent of the word claque, which means a group of people hired to applaud or heckle a performer or public speaker. So the very nature of a clique is to demoralize an individual. In essence a clique is many rejecting one.

The thought that people ignorantly reject others, grossly misrepresenting the God of love, should break our hearts. Where favoritism lifts one person above another, cliques elevate a group to the exclusion of others. Cliques in the church make God's inclusive family seem exclusive and only for special ones. This implies that those who are saved or an acceptable part of the community have somehow earned it. The root is pride, believing that God doesn't call "whoever will may come" (Revelation 22:17) but "whoever fits in."

In racially divided South Africa, from 1948 until 1994, apartheid pitted one people against another. It established a hierarchy of bigotry where the *white clique* excluded other ethnicities.

Even in modern India, the *Bhagavad Gita,* or Hindu scripture, divides people into four groups or castes: the *Brahmins* (teachers, scholars and priests), the *Kshatriyas* (kings and warriors), the *Vaishyas* (agriculturists and traders), and *Shudras* (service providers and artisans). Another group of untouchables are considered outside of the caste system altogether.

John writes in a vision of the equity of God, "And I saw another angel flying through the heavens, carrying the everlasting Good News to preach to the people who belong to this world—to every nation, tribe, language, and people." (Revelation 14:6)

He further describes the inhabitants of Heaven singing of the mighty liberty Christ's death purchased, "And they sang a new song with these words: 'You are worthy to take the scroll and break its seals and open it. For You were killed, and Your blood has ransomed people for God from every tribe and language and people and nation.'" (Revelation 5:9) "He who is the faithful witness to all these things says, 'Yes, I am coming soon!' Amen! Come, Lord Jesus!" (Revelation 22:20)

## CHURCH CLIQUES

The selfishness of cliques within a local church might be more subtle than the splits between races and nations, but they still wound souls.

Our *Church Wounds Survey* found that nearly 29 percent of respondents listed church cliques as the reason behind their scars. Cliques were number seven among church issues with which people struggle. It is far from a peripheral problem.

One survey respondent recounted the past pain of "not being asked to do things because you were not in the cliques." Another twenty-something added, "Cliques in all churches I have been to, especially in youth groups, always existed, but some more than others. It's different when it exists among adults. It's a childish behavior." But the pain inflicted by cliques is far from childish.

Over and over again people shared how church cliques had really hurt them. They simply wanted to feel connected. Yet many felt rejected, left out, abandoned and lonely. In many cases, it was not the senior leaders themselves who were most guilty of alienation. However leadership, or lack thereof, allowed such divisiveness.

The Book of Jude speaks of those who create "divisions (separations) among you. They live by natural instinct because they do not have God's Spirit living in them." (Jude 1:19b)

John writes in his third epistle about a church leader named "Diotrephes, who loves to have the preeminence among them, [and] does not receive us." He loved being first—making others feel less than valuable. How sad!

Jesus warned of the folly of this attitude. "And so it is, that many who are first now will be last then; and those who are last now will be first then." (Matthew 20:16)

He further added, "The greatest among you must be a servant. But those who exalt themselves will be humbled, and those who humble themselves will be exalted. What sorrow awaits you teachers of religious law and you Pharisees. Hypocrites! For you shut the door of the Kingdom of Heaven in people's faces. You won't go in yourselves, and you don't let others enter either." (Matthew 23:11–14)

At times we can forfeit the sublime for the silly, the profound for the petty. One woman wrote of a clique she called "fashionistas who rule the day," adding, "if you weren't wearing the latest trend it was hard to fit in." Being accepted or rejected based on clothing is an obvious example of how superficial cliques really are.

### DOUBLE ANGELS

The writer of Hebrews wrote about at least one reason for having an in-clusive heart, rather than exclusive. "Keep on loving each other as brothers and sisters. Don't forget to show hospitality to strangers, for some who have done this have entertained angels without realizing it!" (Hebrews 13:1–2)

Does God really send angels our way to test the genuineness of our love?

Apparently He does!

Let's carry this point to its logical conclusion. God intentionally sends angels to Earth, in disguise, to provide an attitude check for His people. An incessant complainer, an unkempt undesirable, or an opinionated know-it-all may come our way. All along God is merely testing our willingness to love as He loves.

Yikes!

This gives a whole new meaning to "don't judge a book by its cover."

Why? Because God, who authored every "book," planted somewhat unrelatable "manuscripts" among us so we can read the true character of our hearts and know His.

Even more unsettling and challenging than the possibility of an angel being a double agent are the words of Jesus.

Jesus said, "For I was hungry and you gave me nothing to eat, I was thirsty and you gave me nothing to drink. I was a stranger and you did not receive me as a guest, naked and you did not clothe me, sick and in prison and you did not visit me. Then they too will answer, 'Lord, when did we see you hungry or thirsty or a stranger or naked or sick or in prison, and did not give you whatever you needed?' Then he will answer them, 'I tell you the truth, just as you did not do it for one of the least of these, you did not do it for me.'" (Matthew 25:42–45)

Is there a greater incentive to love at all times than this principle?

Things are not as they appear.

It will take pure hearts and motives to discern His ever-expanding plan.

Some of us may more easily relate to the struggle of embracing a person we regard as less than us, but what about loving the individual we regard as more than us? The Pharisees killed Jesus because they envied Him. (Mark 15:10) We too can distance ourselves from people because we are not willing to accept the unique gifts, abilities or even character they possess.

Paul the Apostle was chosen to take God's "message to the Gentiles and to kings, as well as to the people of Israel." (Acts 9:15) At times we may be called upon to speak to kings of industries, cities, and even neighborhoods—the up-and-outers, not just down-and-outers within our culture.

## A GOLDEN INSIGHT

In what way have we been the masterminds behind our own cliques?

Have people always felt included and accepted around us?

I recently officiated a marriage ceremony between a young deaf woman and a man without any hearing impairment. There are many unique dimensions to their relationship.

Having considered her for about a year before even meeting her, he then spent five hours in a coffee shop with her—writing notes. Falling quickly in love, he learned to sign in two weeks, a timeframe completely outside the norm. You could say he was inspired.

Shortly after their relationship began, they ran into a couple of friends at a coffee shop. While he chatted with them she stood awkwardly to the side, feeling completely left out. Later she confided how uncomfortable she had been during the exchange. Being a sensitive, caring man, from that moment on, he promised to never again leave her out. As of this writing, he never has.

Why would he be so considerate? Why would he promise to never exclude her just because he wanted to include someone else? Because of love! He wanted to care for her as he would for himself. (Luke 6:31) Each of us have felt left out and overlooked, even rejected. To say it didn't feel good would be an understatement. In many cases we can remember where we were standing when the uncaring words or actions took place.

Though cliques come in all sizes, their effect is the same. We all want to be accepted and loved. When we are not, it really hurts. We had hoped to be regarded and valued, but instead felt discarded and devalued. If we can fully capture the pain inflicted by these blatant insensitivities, we will find the incentive we need to never again overlook others.

There are no cliques in Heaven.

May Heaven come to Earth!

# ELITISM

## CHAPTER TWENTY FIVE: *David Loveless*

Many years ago, I invited some dear friends to fly to Dallas to meet up with my wife and me at a Christian conference. Fifteen thousand people had gathered to hear messages from an assortment of the Kingdom's "who's who." One night before the main session, I told our friends we needed to meet the evening's keynote speaker, someone I had recently been introduced to and had ministered with.

After chatting with this speaker, he insisted I join his entourage in the VIP section. Now, I was not even a fly in the soup of this guy's world. To know that this big shot I admired was interested in me made me feel, well, special. Clearly, I had a decision to make. Should I sit with the speaker or go back to my friends? If you had been given this opportunity what would you have done?

Simply put, elitism is a person or people who take pride in belonging to a select or favored group. For those who claim to follow Christ, it is an ungodly form of cliquish snobbery. It divides brothers and sisters by someone's arbitrary idea of spiritual segregation. Countless are the wounds it inflicts. And countless are the centuries the Church squanders in fruitless debate and alienation. We see it all the time in one way or another:

- Protestants judge Catholics
- Pentecostals disdain Evangelicals
- Futurists rebuff ancients
- Liturgicals frown on non-liturgicals
- Young generations dismiss older ones
- Small churches condemn large ones

- Post-moderns mock contemporaries
- Missional churches snub attractional ones

...or vice versa for any of the above, on and on into eternity.

No doubt, at some point you have identified with one or more of these groups and found yourself feeling smug on the inside track. I certainly have.

## WE'RE NUMBER ONE

For all the great things about the denomination I grew up in, among its faults was an unhealthy pride. The largest group of Protestant churches in the world, it constantly hoisted scripture as a beacon of truth to all erring denominations. When I found myself studying for the ministry I was regularly reminded by the faculty and school literature that I was a part of the world's largest evangelical seminary. The arrogance does not belong to this denomination alone. I have lost count of the number of "first" churches I have been a part of or associated with over the years. What is it in us that finds it necessary to perpetually announce through our name, "we were here first?"

After a long day of speaking on the road I went to my hotel room. My brain needed a drain so I switched on the television and saw the pastor of a large congregation teaching about the Christian Church. As I tuned in he was categorizing churches. He talked about 'buffet-style' churches that cater to whatever people want. He talked about 'kiddy-pool' churches, the ones with little spiritual depth. Then he added a whole list of other offending churches and shouted, "Thank God, our church is not like any of those!" The congregation erupted in cheers. I nearly lost my dinner.

Once again this we-know-better-than-you attitude was being perpetuated over the airwaves. But who am I to judge? I too have participated in various forms of elitism and it grieves me to think of it. Every time leaders and their followers tear down other churches, they further dismember the limbs of an already injured Body of Christ.

God led the Apostle Paul to establish this brilliant truth:

*"In Christ's family there can be no division into Jew and non-Jew, slave and free, male and female. Among us you are all equal. That is, we are all in a common relationship with Jesus Christ. Also, since you are Christ's family, then you are Abraham's famous 'descendant,' heirs according to the covenant promises."*
*(Galatians 3:28–29, The Message)*

In Christ's family there can be no division.

Yet, in our need to feel special, we have all fostered elitism. It happens slyly and in the simplest ways. Like when we speak ill of someone who promotes a book espousing spiritual concepts with which we disagree. We exemplify elitism when we think less of someone who supports a ministry or teacher we feel we have some right to "have problems" with. We promote an elitist attitude when we talk about the preferred way we run our family or marriage or business, a way that seems light years better than most. When we do this we tear away from people. We separate us and our kind from them and their kind. We sacrifice unity so that we will not be tainted or tempted to compromise our special status in God's eyes.

Elitism also happens when well meaning Christ followers politicize their Christian values and beliefs. While I've appreciated brothers and sisters who fight to turn the tide of darkness in our culture, so often the actual outcomes of their rhetoric have been divisive, unloving and condemning. In the world's eyes, Jesus is guilty by association. Instead of building bridges, drawing people to Him, we feel it our solemn duty to set the record straight. Along with this has risen a sort of American Christian nationalism that views the United States as God's favored country. We think this while holding up signs at rallies and ballgames with a famous scripture that begins:

"For God so loved the *world*…"

Christian education is often a prime propagator of elitism. Even the best schools fall prey to an our-school-is-better-than-yours mentality. And it's not just on the athletic field. Teachers, administrators, parents and their children often cultivate a nasty form of elitism by the way they talk about and act toward those that have chosen any other mode of education.

Historically, certain powerful church leaders have cornered the market on properly interpreting God's Word. Errantly speaking, they insist only they could obtain God's forgiveness for the people's sins. As a result the Church languished in spiritual darkness for hundreds of years.

## MOST FAVORED NATION STATUS

The New Testament Hebrews were bred to view themselves as God's chosen people. Had not God Himself called them this? Yet at the inception of The Church, the Holy Spirit led Paul, a Jews' Jew, to write in Romans chapter three:

> *"So what difference does it make who is a Jew and who isn't, who has been trained in God's ways and who hasn't?*

> *"Do we Jews get a better break than the others? Not really. Basically, all of us, whether insiders or outsiders, start out in identical conditions, which is to say that we all start out as sinners. Scripture leaves no doubt about it: There's nobody living right, not even one, nobody who knows the score, nobody alert for God. They've all taken the wrong turn; they've all wandered down blind alleys. No one's living right; I can't find a single one.*

> *"And it's clear enough, isn't it, that we're sinners, every one of us, in the same sinking boat with everybody else? Our involvement with God's revelation doesn't put us right with God. What it does is force us to face our complicity in everyone else's sin.*

> *"The God-setting-things-right that we read about has become Jesus-setting-things-right for us. And not only for us, but for everyone who believes in him. For there is no difference between them and us in this. Since we've compiled this long and sorry record as sinners (both us and them) and proved that we are utterly incapable of living the glorious lives God wills for us, God did it for us. Out of sheer generosity he put us in right standing with himself. A pure gift. He got us out of the mess we're in and restored us to where he always wanted us to be. And he did it by means of Jesus Christ.*

> *"So where does that leave our proud Jewish insider claims and counter-claims? Canceled? Yes, canceled. What we've learned is this: God does not respond to what we do; we respond to what God does. We've finally figured it out. Our lives get in step with God and all others by letting him set the pace, not by proudly or anxiously trying to run the parade.*

*"And where does that leave our proud Jewish claim of having a corner on God? Also canceled. God is the God of outsider non-Jews as well as insider Jews. How could it be otherwise since there is only one God? God sets right all who welcome his action and enter into it, both those who follow our religious system and those who have never heard of our religion. (Romans 3, The Message)*

When we first launched Discovery Church, we did so with a conscious effort to be different. What we believed Orlando really needed was not another copy of the same church format repeated for the five hundredth time but a uniquely functioning body, one that carved a fresh path. At the time we did not necessarily think our city needed a better church, we just hoped to make a significant difference in our corner of it. Along with the unchurched population in our area we hoped to help those who rejected God because someone somewhere had imposed a yoke of religious tradition. We saw ourselves as a much-needed alternative.

So we set out to look, sound and reflect "radically different."

Our zealous plan included removing the steeple from the roof and the organ from the sanctuary (we also axed the name sanctuary). We got rid of the choir loft, the pews, the hymnals, and the faux stained glass, even the old, wooden offering plates. Then we dismissed the board of deacons, the traditional Sunday school, a K–5th grade Christian school, and the Wednesday night services. While we were at it we shed our coats and ties and anyone that still did not get what we were up to.

On the plus side we added drums, guitars, synthesizers, circle dancers, mimes, actors, prayer rooms and prayer counselors, elders, two hour-plus worship services which included intense calls for repentance and deeper discipleship. We made room for expressions of spiritual gifts and their accompanying manifestations. We added even more in-depth teaching, fervent discipleship groups and a type of leadership training some referred to as our special forces.

Over time we became the few… the proud… the elite.

Somewhere in our metamorphosis I began to refer to *those other churches* noting (though not by name) that most seemed unwilling to make the costly changes to true discipleship as we had. I talked about *those other churches* stuck in inauthentic and ineffective tradition. Before long, I led many in our church to believe and sometimes state that we were indeed the best, true church in town. You bet we were set apart. We might even be unsurpassed. We made God proud.

But it wasn't God who was proud.

How many times have you felt you had, or felt your church or Christian group had, a "corner on God?" The times we revel in either God's favor or revelation we negate the commands of Jesus that all his disciples live, work and act as *one*. Whether we realize it or not, we foster the very alienation that stalls progress for the cause of Christ. Alienation divides the brethren between the haves and the have-nots. Nothing could be further from the Father's heart. Though, like an earthly father with many kids, God loves each child uniquely, He also shuns all appearance of favoritism.

James illustrates it this way:

> *"For if a man comes into your assembly with a gold ring and dressed in fine clothes and there also comes in a poor man in dirty clothes, and you pay special attention to the one who is wearing the fine clothes, and say, 'You sit here in a good place,' and you say to the poor man, 'You stand over there, or sit down by my footstool,' have you not made distinctions among yourselves, and become judges with evil motives? But if you show partiality, you are committing sin and are convicted by the law as transgressors." (James 4: 2–4, 9, NAS)*

### HEALING FROM ELITISM

That night in the arena I decided to sit with the VIPs. As I did, I waved up to my friends in the nosebleed section hoping they would understand the importance of the moment. They did not. After the conference our friends were nowhere to be found and sadly they have been AWOL from our lives ever since.

I can't tell you how much I regret the decision I made that night. Though later I saw the dark, selfish motive of my heart and asked our friends' forgiveness, our relationship has never been the same. My need to feel special, set apart, above the rest, cost me a most meaningful friendship.

That experience marked me for life. I determined, by God's grace, I would not stoop to elitism again. My behavior resulted from the sin of superiority. I have repented countless times over this, but most importantly, I have invited the Lord to do a major overhaul on my attitude so I can better reflect the Leader of my life. With Christ as my strength I purpose to live out Philippians 2:3–11.

> *"Put yourself aside, and help others get ahead. Don't be obsessed with getting your own advantage. Forget yourselves long enough to lend a helping hand. Think of yourselves the way Christ Jesus thought of Himself. He had equal status with God but didn't think so much of Himself that He had to cling to the advantages of that status no matter what. Not at all. When the time came, He set aside the privileges of deity and took on the status of a slave, became human!*
>
> *Having become human, He stayed human. It was an incredibly humbling process. He didn't claim special privileges. Instead, He lived a selfless, obedient life and then died a selfless, obedient death—and the worst kind of death at that—a crucifixion. Because of that obedience, God lifted Him high and honored Him far beyond anyone or anything, ever, so that all created beings in heaven and on earth—even those long ago dead and buried—will bow in worship before this Jesus Christ, and call out in praise that He is the Master of all, to the glorious honor of God the Father."* (Philippians 2:3–11, The Message)

No matter how many times I read this passage it still rocks me. Jesus was and had every right to be equated with God. In all perfection He was the elite of the elite, yet He chose to walk among us as a commoner. He intentionally chose to associate with the non-elites of His day to make a vital point. His thoughts are not our thoughts and His ways are definitely not our ways. And I will spend my life bending my heart to imitate His.

These days, when I am tempted to act or think as an elitist, I invite Christ to come and pour His humble heart inside me. I intentionally look for the last seat—the back seat either figuratively or literally—to put myself in His place. I rethink comments said to me to make me feel better than someone else and I hang around normal people who love to remind me what a regular guy I really am.

When I encounter others behaving like elitists I remind myself that I too have done that, said that, and thought that. I smile, forgive them and ask God to gently redirect them toward humility. I tell myself that God has His own ways of dethroning elitists. Though sometimes I would like to apply discipline, it is officially God's job. He has something else assigned to me.

I must never forget, the only elite Person in the Universe humbled Himself, and "made Himself nothing." (Philippians 2:7a) Reflecting this God who is love, we must realize "love does not parade itself, [and] is not puffed up." (1Corinthians 13:4, NKJV)

I am pursuing my true identity.

I am pursuing the heart of God.

CHURCH POLITICS

*Section Seven*

# CHURCH
# POLITICS

## CHAPTER TWENTY SIX: *Francis Anfuso*

*"A constantly squabbling family disintegrates."* —Mark 3:24a, The Message

Politics stole my childhood.

In the same year my father ran for the first of five terms as a U.S. Congressman, my mother became pregnant with my twin brother and me. Being in his early forties, and consumed with a political career, my dad was less than excited about this unexpected addition to his family.

He told my mother to get an abortion by taking miscarriage-inducing pills.

She told him to take them.

The birth of my brother Joseph and me was, for my father, a burden to tolerate, not a dream to embrace. By the time Joe and I were five years old, we were whisked away every summer for two months of camp. Nine consecutive years found us there. At barely eleven, we were sent to boarding schools and never lived at home again.

Blatant rejection by my father provided all the reason I needed to disdain him and the politics he adored. The church politics I experienced later in life only added to my distaste.

### THE POLITICS OF RELIGION

Mahatma Gandhi wrote, "Those who say religion has nothing to do with politics do not know what religion is."

One of the reasons people link the words "politics and religion" together is because, at times, they seem indistinguishable. Certainly this was the case in the days of Jesus. At that time political infighting was commonplace for many religious leaders. "Some of the Pharisees said, 'This man Jesus is not from God, for he is working on the Sabbath.' Others said, 'But how could an ordinary sinner do such miraculous signs?' So there was a deep division of opinion among them." (John 9:16)

King Herod wanted to see Jesus. He hoped to see a miracle. In the end he caved to the crowd, the politics of expediency, and crucified the Savior of the world. (Luke 23:8) Though Herod liked listening to John the Baptist (Mark 6:19), he bowed to political peer-pressure, the seduction of a lewd dance and chopped off his head.

It will cost us to stand when others bow.

One of the functions of truth is to separate the real from the phony. As light scatters darkness, so truth dispels lies. "Then God said, 'Let there be light, and there was light. God saw the light, that it was good; and God divided the light from the darkness. God called the light Day, and the darkness He called Night." (Genesis 1:3–5, NKJV)

In every generation God continues to separate light from darkness. "I hear that there are divisions among you when you meet as a church, and to some extent I believe it. But, of course, there must be divisions among you so that you who have God's approval will be recognized!" (1Corinthians 11:18–19) This separation must be based upon biblical truth, rightly interpreted and washed in love, not distorted by the letter of the Word that only kills. (2Corinthians 3:6)

One of the weapons wielded by church politics is the death-imparting letter of God's Word. When we focus on the letter and not the Spirit of the Word, we depart from God's heart using the "out of context" Word of God to justify our under- or overreaction. Our slicing and dicing has no correlation to the divine intent, so clearly stated by Paul to Timothy, "the aim of our instruction is love that comes from a pure heart, a good conscience, and a sincere faith." (1Timothy 1:5, NET) Our aim must never be, "I told him," which only means we never heard from God to begin with.

Dissentious schisms amongst God's people are the enemy of God's plan for a united family. In fact, He hates this divisive spirit and "a person who spreads discord among family members." (Proverbs 6:19, NET)

But division in the family of God continued in the Book of Acts. "This divided the council—the Pharisees against the Sadducees—for the Sadducees say there is no resurrection or angels or spirits, but the Pharisees believe in all of these. So a great clamor arose." (Acts 23:7–9a)

God is not the author of clamor and confusion, but of peace. "And the fruit that consists of righteousness is planted in peace among those who make peace." (James 3:18, NET)

The fruit of God's Spirit produces peace, not politics.

## POLITICS AS USUAL POLARIZES

I have experienced firsthand the pain of being divided from my closest friends. As a church elder, I came close to a nervous breakdown when overbearing leadership disallowed a differing perspective. I felt branded and ostracized. I wish I could say my dilemma was the rare exception.

One man in the *Church Wounds Survey* wrote:

> *"Basically a coup was started against the Pastor I dearly loved. He wanted to take the church in a new direction that I believed was more Christ-like and less legalistic, dissolving the Christian country club environment by moving believers out of their comfort zones and into true service. The 'old guard' in the church, stuck in its rigid ways, refused and, instead of openly discussing objections, it secretly undermined his authority and ousted him. I was disgusted, having attended that church for 17+ years. I have many friends there but I did not want to be a part of that 'body' anymore if their goal was not to be more Christ-like. Ironically, the same thing happened to my father, a retired Baptist Music Minister, when I was 12. He landed where God could use him by becoming a teacher in public schools for the next 25 years and introduced hundreds, maybe thousands, of unchurched and unsaved youth to Christ."*

Admitting he was mostly healed, he courageously concluded:

> *"I have forgiven them. Most of them still do not see anything wrong with what they did. They are God's to deal with not mine. I am flawed in as many ways. I will not be their judge. God has a plan. Be patient! Forgive!"*

Another man wrote of his woundings.

> *"All are related to a senior pastor who pushed (forced) the congregation into building a new sanctuary that was not supported or needed. Hiding behind 'God told me we are to do this,' the pastor would not listen to the leadership of the church and many others in the body who eventually left for other churches. While God has provided a new church home for our family, it hurts tremendously to see the church where my wife and I grew up suffering so much because of one man."*

He added,

> *"I live down the street from the senior pastor. He believes to this day he was right and all of us who disagreed are living in sin. Not much more to say than that. The leadership of the church will ultimately be accountable for the wounds caused. It is not my responsibility to harbor ill will."*

Who will sort all of this out? Only God. In the interim we must decide who's side we're on, God's or our own. They are not the same.


## THE POLITICS OF PAIN

What could be more dangerous than a lie, masquerading as the truth, cloaked in spiritual jargon, in the hands of a leader desperate to be in control? Not much.

Politics and religion are a lethal combination.

Joseph Goebbels, Hitler's Minister of Propaganda, knew the power of both truth and lies: "If you tell a lie big enough and keep repeating it, people will eventually come to believe it…the truth is the mortal enemy of the lie, and thus by extension, the truth is the greatest enemy of the State."

Over the years, I've met many people like myself who were part of churches where so much positioning went on behind the scenes that people became two-faced. A brave new world of spiritual posturing caused many to believe one thing in private and say another in public. It produced an atmosphere of duplicity, phoniness, fear and death.

Winston Churchill once quipped, "Politics is almost as exciting as war, and quite as dangerous. In war you can only be killed once, but in politics many times."

While it is at times painful to be honest, humiliating to be vulnerable, and awkward to yield to God's Spirit, there is no other way to access God. He dwells in unapproachable light. (1Timothy 6:16) Darkness has nowhere to hide in His presence. We must come to the inescapable conclusion—either we willingly choose to unmask darkness in ourselves, or like a virus it will infect every part of our lives.

Marching lockstep with a prevailing political persuasion, whatever the context, may seem painless, but in time disingenuousness always exposes itself for what it really is: fraud. Like Esau of old, we will discern too late, that we sold our future for a bowl of beans. (Hebrews 12:16)

We must not live naïve to the fact that because of our commitment to spiritual integrity we will at times experience the politics of Earth. Plato wrote, "One of the penalties for refusing to participate in politics is that you end up being governed by your inferiors."

If, against our will, we find ourselves subjected to church politics, we must continually remind ourselves: it will only last for a short season. If we resist the seduction to compromise convictions, we will pass the test. We must not lose sight of the eternal reality that by resisting the temptation of political manipulation we receive the deeper joy of honoring the God of Heaven. Raw, real, broken and transparent, we will stand before both God and man with one face—one heart—a whole person. May we fight for that reality!

## GOD'S HEART FOR UNITY

In order to truly represent the pure motive of a holy, humble God, we must be willing to first and foremost bow before Him. Only then can we experience the oneness of heart and mind we each long for. "All the believers were united in heart and mind." (Acts 4:32) This extraordinary oneness, found in the early church, is possible as we "agree with each other, love each other, be deep-spirited friends. Don't push your way to the front; don't sweet-talk your way to the top. Put yourself aside, and help others get ahead. Don't be obsessed with getting your own advantage. Forget yourselves long enough to lend a helping hand. Think of yourselves the way Christ Jesus thought of Himself." (Philippians 2:2–5, The Message)

There are no politics in Heaven. No games. No factions. No two-faces. What you see is what there is: one face, one heart, and one family. The way God intended from the beginning! Birthed in humility! Grounded in trust! The New Heaven and New Earth will be an exact reflection of the One who made it more than possible to be like Him. This was God's plan from the beginning.

God has demonstrated His humble persona in countless ways, but most clearly in the life of Jesus. "You must have the same attitude that Christ Jesus had. Though He was God, He did not think of equality with God as something to cling to. Instead, He gave up His divine privileges; He took the humble position of a slave and was born as a human being. When He appeared in human form, He humbled Himself in obedience to God and died a criminal's death on a cross." (Philippians 2:5–8)

We've been given a glimpse into the every nature of God. He is by nature a humble Servant. His character defers to others. He finds His value by giving value to others.

If God would humble Himself, it must be the essence of who He is. If humility is at the core of His being, then it should be at the core of ours. We were created to be forever joined with both God and one another, in humble, selfless love. "God composed the body, having given greater honor to that part which lacks it, that there should be no schism in the body, but that the members should have the same care for one another." (1Corinthians 12:24b–25, NKJV)

Don't bow to politics!

Don't divide and conquer!

Bow to God alone!

Only then can He conquer every dimension of our lives.

Only then can we share the joy of living victoriously.

# DOCTRINAL DIVISIONS

## CHAPTER TWENTY SEVEN: *Francis Anfuso*

*"If a house is divided against itself, that house cannot stand."* —Mark 3:25, NKJV

Early in the 16th century, a doctrinal difference occurred between two great Christian reformers, the German leader, Martin Luther and the Swiss theologian, Ulrich Zwingli. Though united in their convictions on 14 points, they were unable to agree on the presence of Christ in the Lord's Supper. Zwingli taught that communion is essentially a service of memorial and thanksgiving whereas Luther believed the communion elements were the real and actual presence of Jesus Christ, His body and blood.

Some of us might think, "Who knows and who cares?" Yet these two spiritual giants broke fellowship over this issue. In one of their meetings, discussion literally became a shouting match. Both men later came to their senses and apologized.

These types of divisions are not uncommon throughout church history. At times, doctrinal differences caused breeches. On other occasions relational breakdowns separated those who once walked together. Such a theological division took place in the Book of Acts. "When Paul and Barnabas had a major argument and debate with them, the church appointed Paul and Barnabas and some others from among them to go up to meet with the apostles and elders in Jerusalem about this point of disagreement." (Acts 15:2)

Later Paul and Barnabas faced estrangement as well. Opposed as to whether a disciple named John Mark should accompany them on a mission trip, they parted ways. "Their disagreement over this was so sharp that they separated. Barnabas took John Mark with him." (Acts 15:39)

Though doctrine is certainly important, our *Church Wounds Survey* of over 1,000 participants, unveiled doctrinal differences as the least offensive. This means that, while shepherds may divide over doctrine, it causes minimal wounding of all issues among the sheep. Our default response may be "What do sheep know?" Perhaps they know the true meaning of what Jesus meant when He said, "By this all men will know that you are My disciples, if you have love for one another." (John 13:35, NKJV)

If Jesus meant, "They'll know My disciples by their doctrine," He would have said it. Heart is always higher ground than head. Paul, the brilliant Apostle agreed, "You think that everyone should agree with your perfect knowledge. While knowledge may make us feel important, it is love that really builds up the church." (1Corinthians 8:1b)

## KINGDOM DIVERSITY

Over the past few decades the word "diversity" has increasingly come into vogue. In 2000, the *Magazine Publishers of America* defined it as "recognizing, appreciating, valuing, and utilizing the unique talents and contributions of all individuals."

The essence of this definition is that everyone is valued; all people deserve to be recognized and appreciated. Their unique talents should be embraced and seen for their contribution to the overall good. It's hard to argue against the merits of this open-minded perspective. We should see each person from God's point of view. He is able to wade through our dysfunction and sinful predisposition in order to embrace the "real us."

Our Creator's unconditional love and care for every human being is unshakeable. God demonstrates this depthless love for everyone by giving each of us a priceless part of Himself: the fruits of His character, gifts, talents, personality and passion. The diverse God of the Universe has dispersed His life equally to His creation. We are now left with the question, "Have we used what God has given us to build His eternal Kingdom, or our own?"

We should not seek the benefit of each person's gifts, talents and perspectives for the will of man on Earth, but rather for the cooperation with the sublime will of the God of Heaven and Earth. Until we accept that, in the end, the Creator and Sustainer of all things gets the final say as to what has benefit, we cannot celebrate the most accepting Person who ever lived. The proof of His diversity is evident in that He alone created all peoples, races, and cultures.

## WISE GUYS

Many times, doctrinal divisions come through a battle over "wisdom." The assumption is that the wisest will end up correct before God and man. Here, there is less concern with truth and more concern with being right. But we can never be righteous without the Spirit of God, evidenced in the fruit of peace and joy. (Galatians 5:22) If those aren't evident, God's truth has been contaminated with our flesh.

> *"Mean-spirited ambition isn't wisdom. Boasting that you are wise isn't wisdom. Twisting the truth to make yourselves sound wise isn't wisdom." (James 3:14, The Message)*

> *"But the wisdom that comes from heaven is first of all pure. It is also peace loving, gentle at all times, and willing to yield to others. It is full of mercy and good deeds. It shows no partiality and is always sincere. And those who are peacemakers will plant seeds of peace and reap a harvest of goodness." (James 3:17–18)*

If our greatest commitment is to being right, we should not be surprised if we reap discord instead of peace. Our words should always represent the God of patience and longsuffering, the King of mercy and kindness.

Paul the Apostle established some valid criteria for true Christ-honoring ministry: "We do not give anyone an occasion for taking an offense in anything, so that no fault may be found with our ministry. But as God's servants, we have commended ourselves in every way, with great endurance… by purity, by knowledge, by patience, by benevolence, by the Holy Spirit, by genuine love, by truthful teaching, by the power of God." (2Corintians 6:3–4, 6–7, NET)

### INDISPENSABLE DOCTRINE

Scripture is clear. Sound doctrine is critically important. "All Scripture is given by inspiration of God, and is profitable for *doctrine,* for reproof, for correction, for instruction in righteousness, that the man of God may be complete, thoroughly equipped for every good work." (2 Timothy 3:16–17, NKJV)

It is so essential to our spiritual health that it will be one of the primary battlegrounds in the end times. "Now the Spirit expressly says that in latter times some will depart from the faith, giving heed to deceiving spirits and doctrines of demons." (1 Timothy 4:1, NKJV) We are to be a workman, "who correctly handles the word of truth." (2 Timothy 2:15b, NIV)

The Bible commends those who take the time to research the accuracy of instruction. "And the people of Berea were more open-minded than those in Thessalonica, and they listened eagerly to Paul's message. They searched the Scriptures day after day to check up on Paul and Silas, to see if they were really teaching the truth." (Acts 17:11)

We want to be thoroughly equipped for every good work. No one wants to believe doctrines of demons. Therefore, we must search the Scriptures each day in order to know the truth well.

If we do these things will the fruit of our lives be fully pleasing to God?

Not necessarily.

God is first and foremost looking for those who worship Him in spirit and in truth. (John 4:24) Truth shared with the wrong spirit ceases to bring worship and glory to God. Though doctrine is certainly one indicator of healthy fruit, cultivating the proper attitude or spirit is vital as well. We must speak the truth in love (Ephesians 4:15), not club people with words.

James and John wanted to call down fire upon the villages that wouldn't welcome Jesus. "But He [Jesus] turned and rebuked them, and said, 'You do not know what manner of spirit you are of.'" (Luke 9:55, NKJV)

John tried to stop those who were casting out demons because they were not part of their group. "But Jesus said to him, 'Do not forbid him, for he who is not against us is on our side." (Luke 9:50, NKJV) We should continually ask ourselves, "Whose side am I on, mine or God's?"

There's a BIG difference between standing my ground against sin and arrogantly standing against someone with whom I happen to disagree.

### ATTITUDE IS EVERYTHING

In the Book of Acts, Paul and Silas were arrested, stripped, severely beaten with rods, and thrown in jail with their legs in stocks. You could say they were having a bad day. Yet at midnight on the same day, they had the presence of mind and purity of heart to pray and sing hymns to God. What happened next was nothing short of a miracle.

> *"Suddenly, there was a great earthquake, and the prison was shaken to its foundations. All the doors flew open, and the chains of every prisoner fell off! The jailer woke up to see the prison doors wide open. He assumed the prisoners had escaped, so he drew his sword to kill himself. But Paul shouted to him, 'Don't do it! We are all here!' Trembling with fear, the jailer called for lights and ran to the dungeon and fell down before Paul and Silas. He brought them out and asked, "Sirs, what must I do to be saved?" They replied, 'Believe on the Lord Jesus and you will be saved, along with your entire household.' Then they shared the word of the Lord with him and all who lived in his household. That same hour the jailer washed their wounds, and he and everyone in his household were immediately baptized." (Acts 16:26–33)*

Had animosity been in Paul and Silas' hearts toward the Philippian jailer, they could have left him hanging after the jail cell miraculously opened telling him to "Fry in your own grease!" Instead they helped someone who had hurt them. They helped someone stuck believing lies. Isn't that what we should do—especially for those who are fellow followers of Jesus? Even if their error was sin!

"Dear brothers and sisters, if another Christian is overcome by some sin, you who are godly should gently and humbly help that person back onto the right path. And be careful not to fall into the same temptation yourself." (Galatians 6:1)

There is no action anyone can do—no words anyone can say or believe, that can cause me to give up on him, or provoke me to treat him with less than love, kindness, patience and understanding. It is how Jesus has treated me, and, with His help, "I can do all things through Christ who strengthens me." (Philippians 4:13, NKJV)

# CHURCH SPLITS

A good friend and I once conducted a day-long coaching session for church leaders in Japan. Near the end of our time my friend asked the leaders if we could talk about a sensitive subject: the world-altering event of the 1940's between the United States and Japan. A little hesitant, they agreed.

We started by asking how many in the room had relatives who died in the nuclear blasts on Hiroshima and Nagasaki. Every person in the room raised his hand. From this devastating admission came an honest dialogue that brought a fresh realization for us. Effects of those bombs still, in very tangible ways, reverberate into the twenty-first century. Splitting atoms released megatons of destruction on hundreds of thousands of innocent people.

If you have ever experienced a church split you know a much lesser, though similar struggle of spiritual carnage brought about by war in the church. Some inexperienced might ask, "Is it really that big of a deal?" I'm sorry to break it to you, but the majority of people attending Evangelical churches today will experience one or two church splits in their lifetime. That means countless toxic bombs will be blowing up churches in just about every city and country for our entire generation and beyond.

Not surprisingly then, the mention of church splits permeated our survey. Here is one woman's story.

> *"At my former church there was a split over whether or not to have deacons, elders or a combination of both. Before a vote the pastor asked us to pray about our decision. He led a prayer that included his feelings on the matter. The pastor then said that the Lord had told him how the church should be led and if we didn't agree we should not come back. We lost half the congregation over night. They never really recovered and I hear the church might shut down soon."*

I wish I could say our church has been a shining exception to a story like this.

Many years ago one of our staff pastors came into my office to inform me that God had spoken to him about starting his own church. This was a man I cared about and with whom I shared much life-giving ministry. But in recent days we had engaged in disagreements over the philosophy of our ministry and the significance of his particular role in our church.

When I asked where he planned to start this new church he said he had found a place just one mile from our present location! Then he told me he was prepared to take a number of people with him who shared his belief.

What transpired over the next months, even years, left hundreds of well-intentioned, Jesus-loving, church family members feeling wounded, confused and torn. Together we had experienced some of the most meaningful and amazing moments of growth and community. But here we were divorcing. Twenty percent went with one parent, and the rest stayed home with me in post-traumatic stress.

People on both sides, even those who at one time were best friends, no longer spoke. Those who at one time spoke nothing but blessing and encouragement to one another said some of the most horrible things you would never want to hear.

What causes us to act in ways that cause such destructive pain?

### CHURCHES CHANGE

Admittedly, our church was no stranger to change. Often as our understanding of the wine of the Holy Spirit pours over our congregation we adapt our wineskins accordingly. Usually this excites and refreshes people. But sometimes they get stuck believing surely this particular change must be *the way* Jesus intended His Church to function. And sometimes people get tired of constant change and adjustments they have to make. As a result they just plop down on the most comfortable revelation.

In our case, everyone involved loved God. Everyone meant well. But we just saw the future differently. We came to perceive God's leading, His direction and ultimately His heart, differently. There seemed no recourse but to part. In time I came to believe it was the right thing for all concerned. But to be honest, in the moment, I felt betrayed.

After going through this and other painful situations like it, I have come to see that what the enemy means for evil, God redeems for His good. In time, our church returned to health, vitality, and growth. And today, the other church faithfully lives out the calling God gave them.

Throughout history, God has used splits like ours to expand His kingdom.

We also need to acknowledge that a church split can contrive serious damage to spiritual life. It can alter your trust in God, His church and most definitely its leaders. I've heard some say, "If we were more like the New Testament church and its leaders we wouldn't have such problems." Really?

Acts 15 records how God used Paul and Barnabas as a great Kingdom team to make a significant difference in the lives of people and churches. They were doing well together, until one day…

> *"After spending some time there, they were sent off by the brothers with the blessing of peace to return to those who had sent them. But Paul and Barnabas remained in Antioch, where they and many others taught and preached the word of the Lord. Some time later Paul said to Barnabas, 'Let us go back and visit the brothers in all the towns where we preached the word of the Lord and see how they are doing.' Barnabas wanted to take John, also called Mark, with them, but Paul did not think it wise to take him, because he had deserted them in Pamphylia and had not continued with them in the work. They had such a sharp disagreement that they parted company. Barnabas took Mark and sailed for Cyprus, but Paul chose Silas and left, commended by the brothers to the grace of the Lord. He went through Syria and Cilicia, strengthening the churches." (Acts 15:33–41, NIV)*

What happened to all the unity and singing, "There's a sweet, sweet spirit in this place?" Paul and Barnabas had agreed on the significance of their ministry trip but couldn't agree on who should go with them. Just days earlier, God had used them to unify the church and now these two great leaders were completely at odds. Known for his gift of encouragement, Barnabas wanted John Mark on the team.

But Paul declared that John Mark could not join because he had deserted them on an earlier trip. (Hmmm, a church wound?) He was looking for someone who would enhance not distract from the agenda.

This difference created a serious divide. As a result, Barnabas took Mark and went one way. Paul took Silas and went another. Both traveled, still on assignment for the Lord, but they no longer did it together.

When things like this happen, everyone wants to make it about right and wrong. We think, someone *should be* right and someone *should be* wrong. Which was it in this situation? Does it really matter? Most likely each man spoke a clear thread of truth as well as some level of wrong.

So did God use this? When we read church history we realize that even though leaders in God's kingdom keep changing, work continues on. In fact, sometimes it appears He actually uses situations like this to multiply ministries and churches.

Years ago there was just our church. And then there were two!

### THE BETTER WAY

Jesus' prayer in John 17 highlights an obvious priority of the heart of God. "My prayer is not for them alone. I pray also for those who will believe in Me through their message, that all of them may be one, Father, just as You are in Me and I am in You. May they also be in Us so that the world may believe that You have sent Me. I have given them the glory that You gave Me, that they may be one as We are one: I in them and You in Me. May they be brought to complete unity to let the world know that You sent Me and have loved them even as You have loved Me." (John 17:20–23, NIV)

Because the church is the Bride of Christ, Jesus wants Her to reflect the relationship that He and the Father enjoy. Jesus knew His disciples constantly demonstrated disunity. There was evidence of a competitive and selfish spirit among them.

So how do we change this ongoing ego-driven divisiveness among Christ-followers? "Be completely humble and gentle; be patient, bearing with one another in love. Make every effort to keep the unity of the Spirit through the bond of peace. There is one body and one Spirit—just as you were called to one hope when you were called—one Lord, one faith, one baptism; one God and Father of all, who is over all and through all and in all. (Ephesians 4:2–5, NIV)

Paul's appeal for unity focused on fundamental truths intended to call the Church to unite.

> *One body–One Spirit–One hope–One Lord*
>
> *One faith–One baptism–One God and Father*

## PARTING PRINCIPLES

How should you handle a church split? Or, if you're going through very tough issues at the moment in your church, can you help avoid a break up?

- Keep in mind an important relational adage that says: "It's more important to make things 'right' than to 'be right.' Usually we need to prove we are right. Of course, when we do that, we render the other person wrong. And who wants to be wrong? This statement captures the value of unity. Jesus would rather us make things right than prove to be right.

- When encountering sharp disagreements, determine if the schism is over a fundamental belief of orthodox Christianity (the blood of Christ, salvation, authority of Scripture, the above Ephesians list) or a personal preference (style of music, church name change or governance issues).

- Ask yourself if the disputed issue will be all that important in 5–10 years. Will you and others look back and wonder why so much energy and emotion went toward something of secondary value instead of making disciples? Multiple perspectives on church beliefs and functions exist. Scripture does not spell out many of the practical aspects of church ministry which leaves room for much interpretation. A sober assessment of ourselves and our positions on such matters will alleviate troubles.

- Watch your tone. You might make a great case for your position but communicate it and treat others who disagree with you in a very wrong way.

- As you deal with the dispute, remind yourself that those with opposing views are not the enemy. The enemy is the enemy. The Bible tells us that the kingdom of darkness seeks to "steal, kill and destroy." Remember that your real fight is with the forces of darkness, not the forces of opposition.

- Bring in a neutral, outside mediator. See if he can negotiate a win-win solution; one that addresses the greater concerns of both sides.

- If all sides have tried to resolve their differences to no avail, then find a peaceful way to part. "If it is possible, as far as it depends on you, live at peace with everyone." (Romans 12:18, NIV) Remember, one day you will spend eternity with these people. Even though you may not see eye-to-eye, you can nevertheless accept and affirm the value of another's passions and persuasions. If you can't do that now, the first part of eternity may include a "time out" until you can lovingly relate to the others.

Remember, the wounds from a church split can feel like a divorce. Nothing good comes from screaming, shouting, storming out of the house, walking out of the church, or abandoning relationships. If either side actually believes it has won, a deep price overwhelms any possible good.

Not long ago I was in a restaurant in another part of the country. A pastor I had read about recognized and approached me. Now, this guy is a fantastic leader. I have met people from his church who rave about how much his leadership has meant. When I asked how things were going, the pastor described how a group had left his church to start a new one across town. One look in his wife's eyes told just how devastated they were.

I quickly told the pastor how very sorry I was. I could readily empathize with him. Though not then, I knew he would eventually see that somehow, God does make all things beautiful. In His genius, He makes all things, even the most ridiculous, wrong-headed, horrendous ways we deal with one another work together for His good plan and purpose.

The Lord has given me grace to grow from several different types of splits I have experienced in 30 years of ministry. I have learned about myself, relating to others, the church, the enemy, the Father's heart and I hope I am a better man and leader because of it. I know the overcoming power of Christ's love, not only for me, but also for those who have hurt me.

As much as it depends on you, be at peace with everyone. Bless those who misunderstand or cannot see the Church the way you do. That way, even if you do part ways, you still seek to live every moment in unity.

# HEALING

Section Eight

# FULLNESS
# OF HEALING

CHAPTER TWENTY NINE: *Francis Anfuso*

*"So if the Son sets you free, you will be really free."* —John 8:36, NET

During the previous chapters, we have sadly seen that many wounded souls both inside and outside of the church are now *hostile* toward the Christian faith. We have seen that these multitudes have been *hurt* by the words and deeds of Christians. For some, the pain of these misdeeds has *hindered* them greatly. For others God's *healing* process has been activated, but it will take awhile. Having read many hundreds of church wound testimonies, the brightest light of hope rests upon those who successfully navigated past the storms of *hostile* and *hurt*, and though *hindered,* have arrived at the safe harbor of *healing.*

Of the more than 1,000 people who took our online survey, 86 percent said they had received church wounds. Of these, 65 percent said they were significantly healed. Most of these who took the survey are presently in healthy church environments that are aiding in the healing process so this percentage is by no means a reflection of the culture at large. But it does give us hope that if the church can return to being a safe place, people will come and be healed and not hurt.

Here a positive and insightful person realizes that full healing is on its way: "I feel I am healed. But it's like I have a phantom limb or something. My memory won't allow me to fully trust people in the beginning. I have to enter into relationships carefully, and then when I feel it's safe, I allow myself to be vulnerable."

Another hindered, but hopeful soul wrote that she's "sometimes afraid to get too close with others in the church. I know it's probably not going to happen again but I am cautious." She later added, "Love never fails! When

I was in counseling I learned to trust God again. I know that God is love. When I came across that verse, it told me that God will not fail me. God will not abandon me. That was a huge revelation for my broken spirit. I have discovered He is more real to me than before. He has rescued ME. His hands have touched me. It's not all head knowledge anymore; it's experiential knowledge."

May many of you who have courageously read this book find these comforting words to be true for yourself as well.

## A COURAGEOUS PASTOR ASKS FORGIVENESS

The front page of our Sacramento newspaper had a cover story about a pastor of a large, well-established church in our area. As their senior pastor, he stood before his congregation and publically asked forgiveness from two individuals whose stories had garnered national media attention.

The first individual was a young woman who had been asked to withdraw her daughter from their Christian school because the mother was working as a stripper. The other offended person was an African-American, star student who had formerly attended their Christian school. He was not allowed to graduate with his eighth-grade class because his buzz haircut violated school policy.

On that Sunday morning, the broken pastor emotionally asked for their forgiveness. The pastor confessed an unintended betrayal, which caused much pain. As he did, he struggled to control his emotions. He mourned that the letter of the law was applied, instead of the Spirit.

At one point, the pastor left the pulpit, and walked over to embrace the man and his mother. The congregation gave them a standing ovation, with many openly crying. The young man he had offended finally felt he had closure.

Following the service, with tears in her own eyes, the former stripper, expressed how the pastor's sincere apology peeled back feelings of shame and rejection. The pastor and church leaders offered a full scholarship to her two daughters.

There is no doubt the church around the world has caused much pain to believers and non-believers alike. But courageous actions like this pastor's make all the difference. The power of Christ's redemption, restoration and resurrection was seen through this humble leader.

What the enemy meant for evil, God made very good.

## CHANGED HEARTS CHANGE MEMORIES

A couple of years ago, I wrote a book entitled, *Father Wounds, Reclaiming Your Childhood.* It was the culmination of a lifetime of processing my most pervasive pain: being abandoned and rejected by my father. In one chapter, I recounted a broken relationship with a Christian father figure.

> *"When I was a young Christian, one of my former pastors and spiritual fathers was very abusive. I was a leader in his church. He wounded me deeply, openly ridiculing me before the entire church, my friends and my family. So many times, I drove around town listening to worship music while crying uncontrollably. I felt like I was near a nervous breakdown. I couldn't stop crying. Before the ridicule began, God challenged me to respond well, so I remained silent in spite of the accusations.*

> *"Many years later, as the senior pastor of a church myself, I had a dream about him. In the dream, we were driving along in Heaven. It was majestically beautiful with brilliant colors and complete peace. I turned to him in the passenger seat still full of hurt over the things he had said and done. Without any anger or vindictiveness in my heart, I looked into his eyes and asked, 'Why did you do it?'*

> *"His face was sad but steady. Looking down in embarrassment, and then back up into my eyes, a gentle, understanding smile came on his face. Then reaching out and hugging me, he said, 'It doesn't make a difference anymore.'*

> *"And I knew it was true.*

> *"As we hugged, there was an explosion of love in my heart like nothing I have ever experienced on Earth. The dream ended.*

> *"I woke up sobbing in my bed in the middle of the night.*

*"Some deep, supernatural inner healing had taken place. Though I had forgiven and released him hundreds of times, over many years, I was suddenly freer than I had ever been toward him. It was a glimpse of Heaven and God's forgiving love I will never forget."*

Through this heavenly dream, my relationship with my former pastor was fully healed. Nevertheless, I referred to him as "very abusive." I would modify this harsh description if I were to rewrite the *Father Wounds* book. As surprising as this may sound, the amount of wholeness or un-wholeness in our lives filters our memory. If I am still bitter or angry about a past hurt, then I will speak of the person in question in more derogatory terms. If I have been released from the choking pain of past hurts, then my recollection will be laced with mercy instead of judgment. The actions or words causing the hurt may still be accurately remembered, but the emotional tool they take will be considerably modified.

As the Bible indicates, "For judgment is without mercy to the one who has shown no mercy. Mercy triumphs over judgment." (James 2:13, NKJV) I know I am healed when mercy triumphs over judgment; when my thoughts of people focus more on their need than their offense.

May my mercy for others be new every morning.

### GOD OF MERCY CALLING!

I knew when I set out to write this book that God had fresh and final healing in store for my own Church Wounds.

God did not disappoint.

A few months ago a friend of nearly thirty years approached me saying, "You'll never guess who called me this week!"

The daughter of my first pastor who had caused the severe church wounds I just mentioned had called my friend after decades of silence. I was stunned! God supernaturally facilitated the communication.

Now I had her email address. But it would still take some courage to write her and arrange a meeting. My email was as gracious as possible. Unfortunately, I sent her a section of this book that read, "one of my former pastors and spiritual fathers was very abusive."

I now see the words, "very abusive", as an overstatement. What happened? My own healing has caused me to reflect differently upon my past wounds.

Would the term "abusive" arouse her defenses? Would she even write me back?

Much to my joy she sent me an insightful email, which included:

> *"Dad's generation and the generations before him had its handicaps in fathering. The Holy Spirit revelation of how to father as we understand it now had not been enlightened to them. Our generation almost missed it too, but we have been rescued and can be different with our grandchildren if we didn't make it in time for our own kids.*

> *"If dad had been blind we would have led him. If he had been confined to a wheel chair we would have pushed him. Whatever his generation's fathering handicaps were, we needed to make allowances for it. So, our family decided a long time ago not to let his handicap become our handicap, but serve him, and in that way serve Jesus. I think that is what you decided to do also and so, as you said—'it doesn't make a difference anymore!'"*

How absolutely wonderful! My heart was elated! Even now, my heart weeps for joy as I read her profound words.

As I mentioned in the Prologue, after writing the book *Father Wounds,* and preaching a series on each of the chapters, I found myself completely healed from a life-long wounding. My heart is elated, and so liberated I proudly display pictures of my father in my office. Now, I look forward to Heaven even more, when we will all be together with those we love—healed, fully restored: spirit, soul and body.

In an eternity from now we'll all be sitting around a glorious campfire reminiscing about the marvelous things God did in each of our lives during the Battle for Earth. Then, even more than now, we will see clearly that everything, absolutely everything we have been through was well worth the price of admission. For, by then, the Lord Jesus Christ, would have fully rescued, restored and renewed all that was lost, and replaced it with the irreplaceable.

Until then we will believe.

Until then we will forgive.

Until then we will trust Jesus.

# APPENDIX

**ADOLPH HITLER**

Hitler turned against the Christian faith as a teenager, spending the remainder of his life steeped in the occult. Though the Nazi leader did, on rare occasions, carry a Bible, it was merely to dupe the naïve masses into believing he revered its teachings. Any honest examination of his life will reveal his Gnostic, racist, and neo-pagan roots. His obsession with occultism is so well-documented, it needs little comment.

For a thorough analysis of Hitler's obsession with the occult, examine any of the following volumes:

- *The Occult and the Third Reich* by Jean & Michel Angebert
- *Hitler and the Occult* by Ken Anderson
- *The Occult Roots of Nazism: Secret Aryan Cults and Their Influence on Nazi Ideology* by Nicholas Goodrick-Clarke
- *Unholy Alliance: A History of the Nazi Involvement With the Occult* by Peter Levenda
- *The Nazis and the Occult* by D. Sklar
- *The Twisted Cross* by Joseph Carr
- *The Psychopathic God—Adolf Hitler* by Robert G.L. Waite
- *Adolf Hitler: The Occult Messiah* by Gerald Suster
- *The Spear of Destiny* by Trevor Ravenscroft

## JIM JONES

Responsible for the mass suicide in 1978 of over 900 people in Guyana, South America, Jim Jones ended his life in deception, drug addiction, and sexual immorality. It's no surprise that within the entire Jonestown complex there was not one Bible.

Jones believed that traditional Christianity was a "fly away religion," saying it taught about a "Sky God" who was no God at all.[1] Jones also wrote a booklet entitled *The Letter Killeth*, which ridiculed the Bible.[2] Jones believed he was the reincarnation of Jesus of Nazareth, Mahatma Gandhi, Buddha, Vladimir Lenin, and Father Divine. In a documentary "Jonestown: The Life and Death of Peoples Temple," former Temple member Hue Fortson, Jr. quoted Jones as saying, "What you need to believe in is what you can see... If you see me as your friend, I'll be your friend. If you see me as your father, I'll be your father, for those of you that don't have a father... If you see me as your savior, I'll be your savior. If you see me as your God, I'll be your God."[3]

Two years before his suicide, Jones acknowledged he was an atheist.[4]

---

1    (Wessinger, Catherine. How the Millennium Comes Violently: From Jonestown to Heaven's Gate. Seven Bridges Press, 2000. ISBN 978-1889119243.)

2    (Jones, Jim. "The Letter Killeth." Original material reprint. Department of Religious Studies. San Diego State University.)

3    (Jonestown: The Life and Death of Peoples Temple. American Experience, PBS.org.)

4    (See, e.g., Jones, Jim in conversation with John Maher, "Transcript of Recovered FBI tape Q 622." Alternative Considerations of Jonestown and Peoples Temple. Jonestown Project: San Diego State University.)

## TIMOTHY MCVEIGH

"If I'm going to hell," he wrote, "I'm gonna have a lot of company."[5]

McVeigh consented to a cyber interview with CNN's Lou Michel who later wrote a book entitled, *American Terrorist: Timothy McVeigh and the Oklahoma City Bombing*. Michel spent hours interviewing McVeigh and wrote: "McVeigh is agnostic. He doesn't believe in God, but he won't rule out the possibility. I asked him, 'What if there is a heaven and hell?' He said that once he crosses over the line from life to death, if there is something on the other side, he will—and this is using his military jargon—'adapt, improvise, and overcome.' Death to him is all part of the adventure."[6]

## ERIC RUDOLPH

Atlanta bomber, Eric Rudolph, wrote to his mother, "Many good people continue to send me money and books." In another undated letter, Rudolph wrote, "Most of them have, of course, an agenda; mostly born-again Christians looking to save my soul. I suppose the assumption is made that because I'm in here I must be a 'sinner' in need of salvation, and they would be glad to sell me a ticket to heaven, hawking this salvation like peanuts at a ballgame. I do appreciate their charity, but I could really do without the condescension. They have been so nice I would hate to break it to them that I really prefer Nietzsche to the Bible."

---

5    (Borger, Julian. "McVeigh Faces Day of Reckoning." The Guardian June 11, 2001)

6    (USA TODAY, Special Report: "Eric Rudolph Writes Home" by Blake Morrison, 7/6/2005)

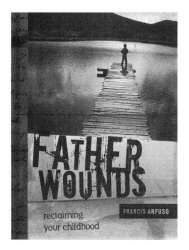

### Father Wounds—
### Reclaiming Your Childhood

As an abandoned and abused son, my soul suffered long-term destruction. But my wounded heart was exactly what God wanted to heal and restore. God can help you forgive the parent who hurt you. He wants to heal you completely and use you mightily in the lives of others!

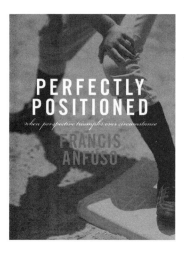

### Perfectly Positioned—When Perspective Triumphs Over Circumstance

Our lives begin to be truly transformed when we stop asking God to change our circumstances and allow Him to change our perspective! Behind every challenging situation there is a loving God whose victorious perspective is far greater than the trials we face. The breakthrough you're longing for is just ahead!

## Living Perfectly Positioned

This book could be called: "The Greatest Hits of Perfectly Positioned." The best of the best revelations are in bite-size, one-a-day pieces. Instead of wishing you had a different script for your life, God can renew your mind to enjoy the only life you have. By changing your perspective, you will see your life changed! God's will is that we would embrace the life He has given us, instead of wishing for what does not exist and would not satisfy even if it did.

## 2029—Church of the Future

Will the Christian church in the western world survive? How does it keep from becoming completely irrelevant? What will the Church of the Future look like? What is about to unfold, and what part will you play?

Order books and audio books online at *www.rockofroseville.com*

Find video clips of Francis Anfuso online at *www.rockspots.tv*

## RECOMMENDED VIEWING

Rockspots

Find video clips of Francis Anfuso online at: www.rockspots.tv.